PORTRAITS OF AMERICA

THE
PACIFIC
NORTHWEST

MARY BRANDT KERR

CHARTWELL
BOOKS, INC.

A QUINTET BOOK

Published by Chartwell Books Inc.,
A Division of Book Sales Inc.,
110 Enterprise Avenue,
Secaucus, New Jersey 07094

ISBN 0-89009-885-9

This book was designed and produced by
Quintet Publishing Limited
6 Blundell Street, London N7
in association with Footnote
Productions Limited

Art Director Peter Bridgewater
Editor Sheila Rosenzweig
Photographer Trevor Wood

Typeset in Great Britain by
Leaper & Gard Limited, Bristol
Colour origination in Hong Kong by
Hong Kong Graphic Arts Company Limited,
Hong Kong
Printed in Hong Kong by Leefung-Asco
Printers Limited

CONTENTS

INTRODUCTION

Captain Cook landed on the western shore of Vancouver Island, at a place called Nootka Sound, in 1778.

Sixteenth-century European explorers dreamed of an intercontinental waterway that would allow direct passage from Europe to the Orient. Such a passage would cut years off the slow and dangerous route around Cape Horn, enabling merchants to save money and cutting down boredom for crews. A northern route from the Pacific to the Atlantic was reputed to exist somewhere across the unexplored reaches of the North American continent, and the very earliest explorers came searching for an access to that passage along the north Pacific coast.

Although it is disputed by some historians, the Spanish explorer Juan de Fuca is believed to have been the first to sail into present-day Puget Sound sometime in the sixteenth century, searching for the waterway that would cross the continent. In 1579 the English navigator Sir Francis Drake (the Spanish knew him as a pirate), having searched as far north as Vancouver Island for a shortcut home to the Atlantic, landed in a cove just north of what is now San Francisco to make repairs. Drake named the region "New Albion" from the cove north and claimed it for the British crown.

The substantial Indian and Eskimo populations living along the coast remained untouched by further European incursions until the eighteenth century, when Spanish explorer Bruno Heceta appeared out of the mist in 1775. Heceta failed in his search for the waterway but discovered instead the mouth of the Columbia River before sailing north to the Nootka country (now British Columbia), claiming the area for Spain.

Less than three years later, the great English explorer Captain James Cook sailed north along the Oregon coast, missed the Columbia River and the Strait of Juan de Fuca in the fog, and landed at Nootka Sound (British Columbia). Just to complicate the territorial issue, he reasserted the British claim to the region as a kind of "consolation prize" to George III for not having found the Northwest passage. Thus the territorial battle lines were drawn for the later confrontation between the two great seafaring nations, Britain and Spain. Who cared what the indigenous population thought?

Although Cook's voyage failed in its original quest, he did make a discovery of a different kind—one that was to have far-reaching and long-term implications for the Pacific North-

Crater Lake opposite, scooped into the crest of the Cascade Range, is a volcanic caldera formed when the ancient Mount Mazama collapsed over 6,000 years ago.

west. Captain Cook's crew bartered with the Indians for a few beaver and sea-otter pelts. The pelts brought fabulous prices in Europe, and almost overnight the fur-trade frenzy replaced the long, arduous search for the Northwest passage that had until then motivated European explorations. English merchants immediately began to outfit vessels and send them to the region to trade with the Indians.

Then in 1788, a ship flying the flag of the new American republic appeared off Tillamook Bay. Captain Robert Gray was also searching for the Northwest passage, but he found instead a small army of English traders. Loading his own ship with furs, Gray hurried home to Boston via China, becoming the first American to circle the globe. More importantly, the furs alerted Americans to the huge wealth on the other side of "their" continent.

Meanwhile, to strengthen Spain's claim to the territory, Don Esteven Martinez was dispatched to land a small band of colonists at Neah Bay (Washington) in 1791. The Spaniards hoped to head off any Russian claims to the area—Russians being well entrenched to the north in what is now Alaska.

Finding instead upstart English traders in Spanish territorial waters, Martinez confiscated the British ships and brought England and Spain to the edge of war. The Spanish cause was not helped when this first white settlement in what was later to become Washington had to be abandoned after just five months. Shortly thereafter, the Nootka Sound Convention was hammered out in deliberations in Europe. Spain was forced to bow to the superior British naval strength, conceding its claim to exclusive trading rights along the northern coast. In 1792, the English captain George Vancouver arrived off the Northwest coast to enforce the terms of the convention.

The Americans Enter the Search

While the British and Spanish ironed out their differences, the American Captain Gray again

Heceta Head Light **right**, one of the world's most photographed sentinels, guards a rocky promontory along the Oregon coast.

set out to find the Northwest passage. Gray met Vancouver amicably at the Strait of Juan de Fuca before each continued on his way—the Englishman north and the American south. Captain Vancouver went into the Strait to the protected passages of Puget Sound, continuing north through the Strait of Georgia and on to the Queen Charlotte islands before sailing around what is now Vancouver Island and declaring it all under the protection of the British crown. For his part, Gray had rediscovered the mouth of the great river and named it for his trusty ship, the *Columbia*. Then, just for good measure, Gray claimed for the United States all of what was to become the Oregon territory.

While Vancouver and Gray were busy exploring the western coast, the two great fur companies operating out of eastern Canada were pushing into the continent's interior. Seeking an overland route to the Pacific, Alexander Mackenzie, a fur trader with the North West Company, reached the Bella Coola country in 1793, missing Captain Vancouver by only seven weeks. Close on his heels were David Thompson and Simon Fraser, exploring the great rivers which now bear their names and establishing North West Company forts and trading posts along their routes.

Although the Spanish presence was clearly on the wane and the Russians had withdrawn to Alaska, the two largest fur-trading companies, the Hudson's Bay Company and the North West Company, now found an upstart Yankee company on their turf. The Pacific Fur Company, formed by New York merchant John Jacob Astor, wasted no time in mounting expeditions; instead, he dispatched David Stuart to explore the region just south of Fraser's and Thompson's routes. Soon the area along the Columbia River was dotted with Astor's trading posts.

Following the Louisiana Purchase of 1803, President Thomas Jefferson commissioned the Lewis and Clark Expedition to find an overland route to the Pacific. Jefferson wanted careful documentation of all flora and fauna as well as the geography of his new acquisition. But he also wanted to challenge the British preeminence along the west coast by finding an easy route on which to move furs and supplies overland to and from the Pacific. The expedition held immense promise for the young republic. Setting off in 1805, the expedi-

tion successfully charted the Snake and Columbia rivers, found a pass through the formidable Rocky Mountains, and established an overland route to the Pacific that was to change the course of American history.

The Fur Trade

In 1806 hundreds of trappers left Saint Louis to follow the overland trail blazed by Lewis and Clark. American ships set off from Boston to begin extensive trading with the coastal Indians. The British, meanwhile, were becoming increasingly anxious (with good reason) about their toehold in the Pacific Northwest. In a bid to reassert their rights, they declared the Nootka mainland British by right of prior discovery and renamed the area "New Caledonia." The fur trade now promised to bring America and Britain nose-to-nose.

In 1810 Astor sent two groups to the mouth of the Columbia, one by land and the other by sea. The *Tonquin* arrived first in 1811 but its crew quickly met with disaster. The overland expedition, following Lewis and Clark's route, reached the mouth of the Columbia in 1811 and established a fort, now known as Astoria.

But Astor's fort was by no means the first in what was to become the Oregon Territory. In the seesaw of power, the North West Com-

missionaries: in 1834 the Methodist Lees settled in the Willamette valley near present-day Salem and in 1836 Dr. Marcus Whitman and his wife settled near what is now Walla Walla.

Extolling the wonders of the fertile Pacific Northwest in letters home to their mission boards, the Lees and the Whitmans were largely responsible for opening up the region to white settlement en masse. The next ten years saw the vanguard of the great migration of Americans across the Oregon Trail. Undaunted by droughts, floods, cholera epidemics, Indian attacks, and the Rocky Mountains, these pioneers trekked steadily west. The lure of lush valleys and free land grants held too much promise, and by 1847 the yearly cavalcades increased steadily to about 4,500 souls, mostly in families.

The British and the Americans

In 1846 the 49th parallel had been agreed upon as the boundary between British-held New Caledonia and American-claimed Oregon Territory. But the treaty was vague as to the precise ownership of the San Juan Islands, and tempers on both sides became short. The events of June 1859 on San Juan Island are surely some of the more hilarious in history.

That was the year that a British pig wandered into an American potato patch; and when an American farmer shot the offending animal, indignation on both sides rose to fever pitch. Both nations readied themselves for full-scale war.

Fortunately for the prospective combatants, cooler heads prevailed (somebody must have pointed out that it had been a *pig* after all, not a human). Tempers subsided and in 1872 the boundary was finally fixed at Haro Strait with the San Juan Islands officially marked as American territory.

While the infamous Pig War held the spotlight, other areas of serious resentment grew. With the white immigrants overrunning their pastures and hunting grounds, Indian anxieties were increasing. In the fall of 1847, a band

pany had already sent David Thompson overland into the area. Thompson had built the first white settlement, Spokane House, in 1810, just north of the present city of that name. Not to be outdone, Astor's company built the rival Fort Spokane nearby a year later.

By 1812 the war between Britain and the States was heating up and American fur traders, unable to get supplies by sea, abruptly pulled out of the Pacific Northwest, leaving the British North West Company in de facto control. Astor's fort near present-day Astoria was sold to the company, and the Oregon country became a commercial outpost of the British crown.

After the war of 1812, Americans moved back into the region. Adamantly refusing to resign their claims to the Oregon Territory based on prior discovery and settlement, they concluded a joint occupation agreement with Britain in 1818. Britain still claimed the Nootka Territory (New Caledonia, now British Columbia) by right of prior discovery.

Missionaries

The wilds of the Pacific Northwest were not to remain uncivilized much longer. Along with this second influx of American trappers came

Today the remote peacefulness
of Nootka Sound belies its earlier history
when Britain and Spain
came nose-to-nose over territorial claims.

Scattered between Puget Sound and Canadian waters, the 172 islands of the San Juan group **right** offer tranquil charm.

of Cayuse warriors attacked the Whitman mission, killing Dr. Whitman, his wife, and several other settlers. News of the massacre shocked the country. Since 1843, Congress had passed laws and developed instruments of government for the newly formed Oregon Territory. The area between the 42nd and 49th parallels, from the Pacific in the west to the Rockies on the east, was officially designated as the Oregon Territory. Then, because of the rapid growth in white population, the Washington Territory was organized in 1853, reducing the Oregon Territory by about 50 percent.

North of the 49th parallel, Vancouver Island had been declared a British Crown Colony in 1849, controlled in practice by the Hudson's Bay Company. (It had merged a few years earlier with the North West Company on the orders of a British government weary of the companies' disruptive rivalry.) The discovery of gold in the Fraser River in 1858 brought a huge influx of prospectors and settlers to the mainland, and the city of Victoria on Vancouver Island became the main supply port.

In the same year Britain declared the mainland a British Crown Colony as well. But because of the huge cost of maintaining separate governments, the two colonies were merged in 1866 and Victoria became the capital. Queen Victoria herself reportedly chose the name for the new colony: British Columbia. Between 1862 and 1871 the gold rush brought not only a marked increase in white migration, but an increase in the general uproar of the gold fields. The Royal Canadian Mounted Police force was established to bring law and order to the wilds of British Columbia and to instill a little British justice amongst the ruffians. With the promise of a transcontinental railway as well as financial aid, British Columbia joined the new Canadian Confederation in 1871 as a province.

Gold was discovered in northeast Washington in 1855, and that brought a rush of prospectors and settlers there, heightening Indian anxiety. The next four years saw intermittent Indian warfare against the settlers before Chief Seathl made his moving declaration: "My people are few. . . . There is no death. Only a change of worlds." With that, rebellion ended and the Indians were banished to reservations. Oregon became a state in 1859; Washington, in 1889.

With the arrival of the transcontinental railroad at the end of the nineteenth century, the Pacific Northwest was finally opened up. The port cities of Seattle, Portland, and Vancouver charged into the twentieth century on the crest of the Klondike gold rush. Later, world wars brought modern industrialization to the region. And, to soften the full force of the Depression, the Columbia River Project in Washington brought new impetus to the area, forever changing both the economy and the thrust of the Pacific Northwest.

MOUNTAINS AND COASTLINE

The Pacific Northwest is a majestic land sculpted by glaciers and the cataclysmic action of volcanoes. It is a region of unparalleled natural beauty characterized by a long, rugged coastline and towering snow-clad mountain ranges. But it is also an area of deep, brilliantly blue lakes, rain forests almost tropical in their moisture, rivers rich with fish, and valleys of abundance coupled with semi-arid plateaus and canyonlands. It is a region of unspoiled beauty and variety—and its inhabitants today struggle to keep it that way.

Sixty million years ago—yesterday morning in geological time—the massive landscaping of the Pacific Northwest began. It was covered by a prehistoric ocean, but volcanic activity under this ancient seabed began to thrust up a long ridge of mountains stretching from present-day Alaska south to California. Simultaneously, volcanic action threw up lava rock and volcanic ash. The ridge formed as a result of this volcanic simmering was the beginning of the Cascade Range, which effectively split the ancient ocean into an inland sea to the east with the ocean to the west.

As the bottom of the inland sea covering much of this area began to boil up its confined waters sought an escape. The lowest and weakest part of the Cascades eventually gave way to the Columbia River Gorge with its awe-inspiring rapids and precipitous waterfalls.

The dawning of the Ice Age further altered the Pacific Northwest's features. A giant glacier covered most of British Columbia and the Columbia Basin, blocking the Columbia River near today's site of the Grand Coulee Dam. The river was forced into other channels throughout the plateau. As the glacier began to move, pushing rocks and boulders in its path, numerous lakes and coulees were gouged out of the valleys—lakes that we enjoy today as sources of both recreation and irrigation.

Then, about 15,000 years ago, the warming of the earth brought an abrupt and dramatic end to the Ice Age. Melting ice crashed boulders and gravel into the rivers of the Columbia Basin causing them to flood and again carve new channels. Islands were created and huge gulches were formed by the melting ice, the Grand Coulee channel being the most spectacular. Beginning just south of today's Grand Coulee Dam, this channel averaged three miles across as it gouged deeply into the landscape. At the Dry Falls this channel tumbled four hundred feet over a chasm three miles wide—a drop that dwarfs Niagara Falls.

Volcanic activity began again as the glaciers melted, and Mount Rainier was the first to shatter its crest in a belching explosion of volcanic gases. Mount Mazama, in Oregon, erupted next and formed a new crater—today a crystal-blue lake filled by water from rain and snowmelt and known as Crater Lake, a prime vacation spot in the Pacific Northwest. A third explosion, of the now defunct Mount Multnomah also located in southern Oregon, left the Three Sisters sitting atop the rim of its crater, now part of the Willamette National Forest. Mount St. Helens's recent activity gives us a graphic reenactment of what these prehistoric eruptions must have been like. Mount St. Helens also blew away its top 2,000 feet, and the collapse of its cone formed a crater that still bubbles with steam from its summit.

Right "Down these heights frequently descend the most beautiful cascades," noted Lewis and Clark in their expedition journal. It is thought that the name of the Cascades mountain range derives from these numerous waterfalls.

Opposite Mount Saint Helens—the most notorious of the Pacific Northwest's volcanoes—was also one of the tallest until it blew off its top 2,000 feet in the famous 1980 eruption.

South Sister **right** is part of the triumvirate that guards the rim of the ancient volcano Mount Multnomah in Oregon's Deschutes National Forest.

The shimmering snow cone of Washington's Mount Rainier **below left**, seen here from Gig Harbor, towers to 14,410 feet of dormant volcano cloaked in more than 25 glaciers.

During all this "uplifting" activity on the mainland, another mountain range was sinking into the ocean off the British Columbian coast. The San Juan Islands, Vancouver Island, the Queen Charlotte Islands, and countless other islets and humps are the topmost peaks of this now submerged ancient mountain range.

The Cascades

Today the Cascade Mountains form the single most remarkable geographic feature in the Pacific Northwest. Comprised of a range of isolated peaks of volcanic origin—part of the Pacific "Ring of Fire"—the average elevation is around 7,000 feet. At 14,410 feet Mount Rainier in Washington is the tallest, followed by Mount Adams at 12,326 feet (also in Washington), with Oregon's tallest peak, Mount

Rugged coastlines **left**, jagged fjords and sandy beaches characterize the 250 islands forming the Queen Charlotte group. These isles are actually the summits of a sunken range of mountains stretching north from Puget Sound.

A working river **overleaf** as well as a recreational waterway, the magnificent Columbia is second only to the Mississippi on the North American continent.

In contrast to the jagged precipices characteristic of the northern Cascades, alpine flowers mantle these gentle meadows **right** in the southern reaches of the range in Oregon.

Hood, a close third at 11,235 feet. Mount St. Helens in southern Washington was formerly one of the highest peaks until it blasted off its top in the catastrophic explosion of May, 1980.

Extending as it does from northern California into British Columbia, the Cascades also acts as a gigantic climatic barrier. West of this range lies the dramatic coastline averaging 35 inches of rain per year. As you approach the mountains from their western side you find yourself in the lushest of rain forests where giant ferns and dogwood drape the meandering mossy streams. The average annual precipitation ranges from 65 to 150 inches on these western slopes, giving the region its "evergreen" nickname.

Higher up, these western slopes are heavily forested—forests that yield a huge proportion of the timber used in the United States today. Near the summits of these American "Alps" the rainfall increases to some 200 inches per year. In the North Cascades, rows of rugged, steep-walled peaks are worn sharp by the glaciers they still carry. To the south, in Oregon, these same mountains subside into rolling alpine meadows blossoming into a

blaze of color every spring.

Moving east, across the Cascades, the eastern slopes lie in the rainshadow of the mountains. The air here is drier and warmer, receiving a scant six to eight inches of rainfall annually. The dense alpine forests of the western slopes give way to uncrowded stands of pine interspersed with sun-washed meadows.

The pines and meadows in turn give way to the broad, flat, semi-arid plateau of the Columbia River Basin. This vast basin extends from the rainshadowed hills of the Cascades to the Snake River, flowing along the eastern border of Washington, and to the jagged mountain ranges of eastern Oregon and the Canadian Rockies on British Columbia's eastern edge.

The Pacific Northwest boasts several other majestic mountain ranges, in addition to its backbone, the Cascades. British Columbia has the Coast Mountains along its Pacific edge bordered to the east by the province's broad plateau.

Rivers

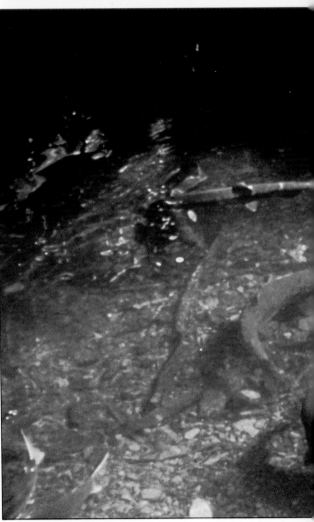

In the middle of its Olympic Peninsula Washington has the Olympic Mountains culminating in towering Mount Olympus (7,965 feet). Puget Sound, with its major cities of Seattle, Everett, and Tacoma, is sheltered in the eastern rainshadow of the Olympics from the worst of the rain. Citizens of these cities don't seem to believe it, however, ruefully adding "ever wet" to the "evergreen" reputation.

Oregon's coast is also closely bounded by the Coast Range. The Willamette River flows through the trough between the Cascades and the Coast Range, finishing its journey to the Pacific as part of the Columbia. In the south this trough between the two mountain ranges forms the Willamette valley and in the north it is Washington's Puget Sound. On Oregon's farthest eastern edge are the lesser ranges of the Blue Mountains, which reach into Washington's southeastern corner, along with the more precipitous Umatilla and Wallowa ranges. The Steen Mountains in the southern

Sheltered in the rainshadow of the Olympic Mountains, Puget Sound **above** is a marine paradise. A large percentage of the people living around the Sound commute daily on its extensive ferry system.

Finding their way home to their shallow nurseries, the sockeye salmon **below** make for legendary fishing. Almost 850,000 pounds of salmon are caught by sport fishermen each year in Washington alone.

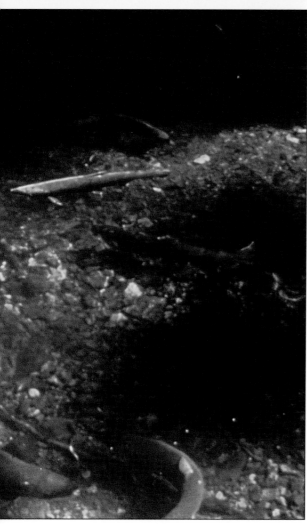

portion of the state form a backdrop for the semi-arid plateaus, broken only occasionally by spectacular gashes and ancient lava beds.

The Fraser River system in British Columbia is the major artery for all interior salmon runs. Salmon returning in their annual "run" use the Fraser to reach their spawning nurseries in the upper reaches of the Thompson, Adams, Quesnel, and Clearwater rivers. Washington has several water arteries including the Spokane and Snake rivers, and Oregon has the Rogue, Umpqua, and Hood rivers in addition to the Willamette. But it is the mighty Columbia, second only to the Mississippi on the North American continent, that really dominates the landscape. Beginning in a lake in the Canadian Rockies, the river flows north, west, and then south before it leaves Canada to enter Washington. Rushing through eastern Washington to the Pacific via the Oregon-Washington border where it steps down a series of steep falls and rapids, the river is today, as it was in the past, a major trade route. It is by forcing the Columbia back into many of its prehistoric channels that modern man has controlled the river for irrigation purposes. Its waters have turned the central plateau from a barren desert, dreaded by the earliest pioneers, into blooming orchards and vineyards.

And this landscaping project is by no means finished, as Mount St. Helens's constant tremors and steam plumes demonstrate. Mother Nature continues her work in the magnificent Pacific Northwest.

NATURAL RESOURCES

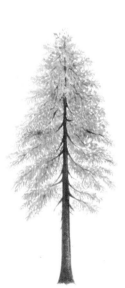

The giant **Douglas fir**, a favorite of the logging industry, is native to the western slopes of the Rockies. It grows to a height of 200 feet and has a powerful, sweet aroma.

Legendary salmon runs lure commercial fishermen, such as these **right** off Port Renfrew, Vancouver Island, as well as sports enthusiasts.

Opposite A clattering heap of trashed shells is a vital tool in the highly commercial business of oyster farming. Strung together on wires or in nylon mesh, these "pre-owned" oyster and scallop shells are the nucleus for growth of future oyster progeny. Oyster larvae—evidence of oyster hanky-panky in July or August—reach their teens by gluing themselves to any hard object—a rock, a boat bottom, an old shell—and quietly growing there. Oyster farmers need to shift this adolescent crop to secondary "pastures" and find it much easier to hoist a rack of "mother shells," with the spats, or pubescent oysters, attached to them, rather than pry each beastie off a rock.

raditionally, the economy of the Pacific Northwest has been dependent on resource-based industries. For example, forestry and the Northwest go hand in hand. Now, new industries like electronics are being wooed, and the resource industries are waning in importance. But forestry is still Oregon's and British Columbia's most important business, whereas in Washington it is a close second to transportation-equipment manufacture. Vast stands of timber, growing mostly along the west coast, yield Douglas fir, ponderosa pine, red cedar, and western hemlock. Oregon, with almost half its acreage forested, is the United States' leading timber-producing state.

Agriculture and fishing rank high too. The northern areas of British Columbia produce wheat and oats, though not in quantities that might worry the plains provinces to the east. Fruit-growing is found in the Okanagan and Fraser valleys, and the center and eastern edge areas of the province are chiefly sheep and cattle ranching country.

South of the border, Oregon and Washington pump out vast volumes of winter wheat, potatoes, onions, and beans from eastern plateaus washed by the Columbia River. Indeed, in some years, Nebraska and Kansas have had red faces as Washington's wheat output has surpassed theirs. Apples, pears, berries, peaches, cherries, plums, and sugar beets thrive in the mild fertile valleys of the Willamette and Hood rivers in Oregon and east of the Cascades in the Wenatchee valley in Washington. Washington is also the nation's leading apple producer.

Among the rolling hills of the coast, from British Columbia to Oregon, the dairy industry is a major factor, with some of the world's most contented cows producing milk and the milk for specialty cheeses for markets worldwide.

It wouldn't be the Pacific Northwest without commercial fishing. British Columbia's rivers and coast produce nearly one-third of Canada's total fish catch. The commercial fishing fleets yield salmon, halibut, and bottom-dwelling fish like flounder; shellfish such as oysters, clams, and crabs are farmed and pro-

In the secondary growing area, correct water temperature, moderate salinity and adequate food supply are essential to build up a growing oyster's bivalves. The grown oysters are eventually harvested by dredge, or rather more laboriously, by hand, as this lady **right** is doing at Hood Canal, Washington.

Skilled pilots maneuver small dories, like this one **left** pictured at Cannon Beach, Oregon; through the surf in pursuit of rich harvests of halibut, flounder and salmon.

cessed in Oregon and Washington, and the tiny pink Alaskan shrimp has recently been found off Oregon to add to the haul. British Columbia's Vancouver, Washington's Seattle and Everett, and Oregon's Astoria, Newport, and Portland are today's major Cannery Rows on the west coast.

Since the late nineteenth century, Mother Earth's underground treasures have added to the region's bounty. British Columbia still produces large quantities of silver and has some of the world's largest zinc and lead mines at Kimberley, on the edge of the Canadian Rockies. Washington and Oregon both mine some lead and zinc too. Gold, copper, and coal are still plumbed from the depths in limited amounts throughout the Pacific Northwest. Recently, Oregon and British Columbia have been blessed with a boom in oil and gas drilling—enough to float a fledgling petroleum industry. And aluminum production is a prime industry; Washington heads the nation's list, followed by Oregon, and across the line, British Columbia has a giant aluminum production site at Kitimat.

The northwest corner is also famous for the manufacture of transportation equipment, in both shipbuilding and aircraft production. Seattle is well known as the "capital" of the Boeing Aircraft Corporation empire; Boeing is the free world's largest manufacturer of commercial transport airplanes. World War II is largely responsible for bringing this industry to the Pacific Northwest, and it continues to be vital for employment and revenues as the economy diversifies and expands. Lately there has been some movement away from aerospace and defense contracts and a shift toward an increased share of the electronics market. Indeed, Oregon already has quite a reputation as a hotbed of high tech, with giant

computer companies like Hewlett-Packard entrenched in Corvallis. Some wags have labeled Oregon's concentration of electronics expertise "Silicon Forest."

Tourism is the final component in the economic jigsaw of the Pacific Northwest; because of the unspoiled environment, recreation here is largely oriented toward the great outdoors. National parks and forests, thousands of lakes and streams, miles of wilderness shoreline, all lure the city-weary vacationer. Among the major attractions are downhill and cross-country skiing; coastal fishing for salmon and bottom fish; freshwater fishing for the feisty steelhead, trout, and bass. And boating, diving, river-running and tide-pool exploration are all possible in the Northwest's abundant aquatic playgrounds.

This pretty little craft **left** moored in South Bend, Washington, is used to net a rich catch of trashed shells.

THE PACIFIC NORTHWEST COAST

ew areas in the world can rival the Pacific Northwest coast for wild, rugged beauty unspoiled by man. From the broad sandy beaches and huge dunes of southern Oregon to the jagged fjords of British Columbia this coast is a land of contrasts and spectacle. For sheer power and moodiness, little in nature can match the great winter storms that lash the beaches. Yet the sea can be calm, encouraging beachcombing and berry picking along its edges. Indeed, hardy natives have even been known to sunbathe (always a relative term in this part of the world) on these beaches.

The **western bluebird**, a sparrow-sized bird distinguishable from the eastern variety by its rust-red beak, frequents open forests and farmland.

Rugged fjords **below** cloaked in stands of spruce line the water's edge at Jervis Inlet in British Columbia—visually reminiscent of Norway.

Opposite "Go fly a kite" takes on a literal meaning on the beach at Lincoln City. Kite flying is so popular in this part of Oregon that several local craftsmen devote all of their talent to the design and constructions of unusual kites.

The Oregon Coast

Driving north from the California-Oregon border the south coast of Oregon includes not only the most urban areas but also its least-explored beaches. The ruggedly beautiful coastline, less populated in the south, offers secluded beaches punctuated only by the scenic estuaries of numerous rivers and streams. Views of forested, grass-covered mountains sloping to the sea dominate the landscape.

In the mid-1960s, Oregonians, ever vigilant against the "Californication" (a word of their own derivation) of their state, were faced with the kind of commercial threat to their beaches that has sullied much of southern California's coast. In an extraordinary move the Oregon legislature passed a bill forever preserving all the state's beaches for "free and uninterrupted use" by the public.

In the very southern section of Oregon's coast, located at the mouth of the Rogue River, lies the town of Gold Beach. Overlapping fishing seasons with huge runs of salmon and steelhead have made Gold Beach an international sportfishing port. The name comes from the fact that feverish prospectors found gold in these sands, and although it was never successfully mined you can still see where deposits were extracted from adjacent hills.

If fishing isn't your sport, the Rogue River offers magnificent wilderness with its deep, forested canyons edged by the 40-mile Rogue River wilderness trail.

Port Orford offers a series of firsts: it is the

The Rogue River, seen **above** at its mouth at Gold Beach, is one of Oregon's recreational paradises, offering white-water rafting, canoeing and jet-boats as well as an historic maritime mail boat.

Splashes of late spring, wildflowers **below** cavort along a bluff overlooking driftwood and tidepools on Port Orford's beach.

westernmost incorporated city in the contiguous forty-eight states, its Cape Blanco (white chalk cliffs named by the Spanish in 1603) is the westernmost headland, and atop that westernmost headland is the westernmost working lighthouse, in operation since 1870. Captain George Vancouver first sighted and named the bluffs here for the Earl of Orford in 1792. Settled in the mid-nineteenth century, the town became a major shipping center for cedar logs—still an important industry. Port Orford has a fine deep-water harbor, making it a busy center of commercial fishing. One of the largest sea-lion colonies congregates just offshore from Cape Blanco,

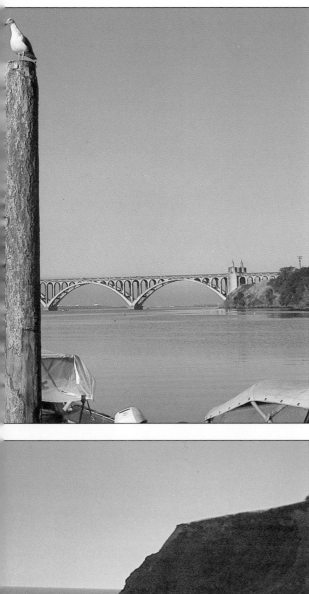

and even in the fog you'll be able to hear their distinctive caterwauling. Historic Battle Rock on the beach at Port Orford commemorates a skirmish between some irate Indians and a small group of white settlers, now faithfully reenacted every Fourth of July, which should give you an idea of which side won.

Continuing north along Highway 101 you come to Bandon, distinguished by rocky outcrops looming over a smooth, sandy beach. Self-proclaimed as the "storm-watching capital of the world," Bandon's Old Town, lying along the waterfront, offers good vantage points. Bandon is also known for its cheese and cranberry industries. Clamming, crabbing, and cranberry picking are a few of the other activities you can try your hand at. Just north of town at Bullards Beach State Park a restored lighthouse is open as a museum. Bullards Beach is also a destination for rock hounds—jasper, agates, and other semiprecious stone proliferate where earlier prospectors searched for gold.

More than 25,000 people live in the three communities constituting the next area along the coast: Oregon's bay area—North Bend, Coos Bay, and Charleston. This is by far the most heavily populated area of Oregon's coast. A major center for lumber and shipping, the bay also offers everything a fishing enthusiast could possibly want in the line of sportfishing, from charter boats to equipment hire, whether it be deep-sea or bay angling. The estuary here has a striped-bass fishery and is a good source of clams and crabs. Sunset Bay State Park offers the safest swimming area along the Oregon shoreline—safe if you don't die of a heart attack from the water temperatures.

Dune Country

North of Coos Bay is Reedsport, in the heart of Oregon's famous dune country. Stretching for approximately 42 miles along the coast these dunes are some of the most spectacular formations in the world—reputed to be larger

Unobstructed views of impressive seascapes begin at the California-Oregon border **left**. Such fine scenery is protected by numerous coastal state parks such as Cape Sebastian **overleaf**.

Sheltered by a sand dune, colorful water plants **right** dot a small pool at Florence, Oregon.

The Heceta Head Light **center** looms majestically over a wind-scoured, wave-lashed beach.

than anything the Sahara can offer. Some dunes attain heights of as much as 300 feet in this ever-changing spectacle.

Nearby is Winchester Bay, formed by the Umpqua and Smith rivers, both of which offer striped-bass fishing expeditions in the spring. When you get tired of fishing or roaring over the dunes, take an interesting side trip up the Umpqua to the frontier mining town of Scottsburg just east of Reedsport. Hunting for deer and bear is possible nearby, and Scottsburg is home to the annual White Water Canoe Race on the Umpqua.

At the mouth of the Siuslaw River is the small city of Florence, an ecological transition point. Here the coastal scenery abruptly changes from a long chain of sandy beaches to heavily forested mountains. Thousands of wild rhododendrons bloom near the city, and Florence's annual Rhododendron Festival, held in May, is a celebration of nature's colors.

Just north of Florence is located one of the

few mainland nurseries for the Stellar sea lions. Driven nearly to extinction, the sea lion has learned its lesson, and most calving nurseries are located well offshore. Here, however, you can watch the pups playing in the surf while 2,000-pound bulls preen and jockey for position on the rocky outcrops. Then a short drive beyond the sea lion nursery brings the visitor to one of the most photographed sentinels on any coast: Heceta Head Light. Named for the Spanish explorer who first charted the treacherous cliffs in 1775, Heceta Light is still an operating lighthouse.

Newport, located at the entrance of Yaquina Bay, offers a large port nationally famous for its Dungeness crab and shrimp fisheries. The bay's tidal flats are also a good source for clams; crabbers need go no farther than the pier. And if it is bottom fish you're after, the waters just out from this bay are teeming with perch and flounder. One of the more unusual attractions of Newport is the

As its name suggests, Oregon's Cape Foulweather **left** offers a ringside seat for watching the Pacific Northwest's moody winter storms. It's also ideal for seasonal whale-watching.

The magnificent sand dunes
of southern Oregon **above** and **right**—their
whiteness shimmering beside
the blue Pacific and forever sculpted by
winds—are said to be more
impressive than the vastness of the Sahara.
Most of the dune country today
is protected by the National Dunes Recreation
Area stretching along the Oregon
coast from North Bend north to Florence.

Mark O. Hatfield Marine Science Center, which features an exceedingly friendly octopus in the handling pool that apparently relishes the chance to "shake hands" with visitors. The beaches just north of Newport are famous agate grounds, and the Yaquina Head Lighthouse—erected in 1871 and one of the first built on this coast—is open to the public.

North along Route 101 is the aptly named Cape Foulweather. British explorer Captain James Cook, using all his creativity, named these spectacular cliffs after having witnessed a typical Pacific Northwestern winter storm. Both Cape Foulweather and adjacent Depoe Bay are good vantage points for storm-watching, wave-watching, and whale-watching.

As you drive north heading for Lincoln City, trivia fans should watch for signs indicating the "D" River, proclaimed by locals as the shortest river in the world. Lincoln City is smack in the middle of Devil's Lake State Park. The town is well known for its excellent kite-flying beaches (happily devoid of any of Charlie Brown's kite-eating trees), and local craftsmen design and construct specialty kites for the real aficionados. The lake, besides offering the usual water sports, also features an annual hydroplane race for speed fans.

Just north of Pacific City is the Three Capes Loop drive connecting three distinctive promontories: Cape Kiwanda, Cape Lookout, and Cape Meares. The Cape Kiwanda area is a mecca for skin divers and tidepool explorers, and a state park trail leads to ocean overlooks. The sandstone cliffs of Cape Lookout with adjacent sand dunes is a favorite jumping-off point for hand gliders. Cape Meares features a restored lighthouse and a short hiking trail through a stunningly overgrown rain forest to a spruce tree appropriately known as the Octopus Tree. The trail culminates with a magnificent view of offshore rocks along the coast.

Garibaldi Rockaway, Twin Rocks, Manzanita and Nehalem (meaning "place of peace") are all small resort communities offering recreational fishing and old-town charm. For the energetic a hike up Neahkahnie Mountain above Manzanita will give you time to contemplate the possibility of a treasure hunt.

Local Indians believed this headland was the home of the supreme god "E-Kah-Ni." The crew from a wrecked Spanish ship chose to capitalize on Indian reluctance to ascend the sacred mountain and buried their treasure on it. Or so the story goes. No treasure has been found, but some partially buried rocks with mysterious lettering carved on them have been uncovered.

North of these small communities lies Tillamook, the commercial center of Oregon's dairy-products region. Cheese fans can tour and sample at any one of several factories here, and anglers have a choice of nine rivers converging into this area. On the other side of Tillamook Head is the arts colony of Cannon Beach. This little town features a summertime series of music and art events as well as an annual sand-castle contest. Kite-flying and surf-fishing are also popular activities here. An offshore wildlife refuge is located on 235-foot Haystack Rock, similar to one off Cape Kiwanda.

On November 7, 1805, Captain William Clark recorded in his diary, "Ocean in view! O! the joy." In fact, the weary overlanders were 25 miles away from the coast at a wide point on the Columbia River. But when the Lewis and Clark group finally dabbled their toes in the surf it was on the wide, sandy beach at Seaside. A lovely old beachside resort, Seaside is complete with a two-mile promenade that features a replica of the salt ciarn that Lewis and Clark built to extract salt from the sea.

North from Seaside is Astoria, the first permanent American settlement in the Oregon Territory. Now a showcase of historic landmarks, museums, and elegant Victorian architecture, modern Astoria is also home to a large commercial fishing industry. Crab, salmon, tuna, sturgeon and several varieties of white fish populate the waters just out of Astoria. The 166-step Astoria column on Coxcomb Hill offers a fine view of the Columbia River with its oceangoing ships, distant mountains, and pastoral meadows below. Several historic forts are nearby. Six miles southwest of Astoria Lewis and Clark built Fort Clatsop as a winter shelter in 1805–1806. In 1811, hardy trappers from John Jacob Astor's Pacific Fur Company built Fort Astoria, from which the modern city derived. And between Hammond and Warrentown is Fort Stevens—built to protect the entrance to the Columbia from

Offshore, rocky outcrops **center** like these near Lincoln City, Oregon, serve as bird and wildlife refuges as well as photographic backdrops.

The Astoria Bridge **left** sweeps north for four miles across the mouth of the Columbia to the Washington town of Megler.

Immediately north of Heceta Head, the 800-foot-high Cape Perpetua **below** offers dramatic ocean panoramas. Several trails lead to cliffside points where visitors can admire the power of the waves as they assault the rocky headland.

At the very southernmost tip of the Long Beach peninsula **overleaf**, just inside the Columbia River mouth, lies the bustling port of Ilwaco. The harbor is home to a fleet of hardy commercial and sports fishing boats.

"He was a brave man who first ate an oyster," declared Dean Swift. If you think you're brave, you can tour South Bend's Coast Oyster Company facilities, seen here **above** behind piles of oyster "mother" shells.

The men of Lewis and Clark's expedition endured such a miserably wet, cold winter in 1805–06 at Fort Clatsop **below** that some of them swore it took several years to warm up again.

Confederate attack. This fort also enjoys the doubtful glory of being the only American mainland fortification to be fired upon in World War II—by a Japanese sub-marine in 1942.

The Washington Coast

The **osprey** makes a magnificent sight as it plunges feet-first into the water to catch a fish.

Across the mighty Columbia lies Washington's coast. From Cape Disappointment in the south of Cape Flattery in the north, it is an area of sheltered coves and bays, forested headlands, and wave-swept beaches. Delightful in summer, this coast's winter storms offer unparalleled drama, and the very northern section of the state's shoreline along the Olympic Peninsula is some of the wildest and loneliest in North America.

At the southern end of Washington's coast lies the Long Beach peninsula, a popular resort area since the nineteenth century. This 28-mile sandspit stretches north from the mouth of the Columbia River to its very tip at Leadbetter Point State Park. The area in between is a kaleidoscope of unbroken beaches, small historical communities, cranberry bogs, some of the world's most prolific oyster beds, and excellent clamming opportunities.

Ilwaco, the southernmost town on the peninsula, is home port to a sizable sportfishing fleet, where you can venture forth in pursuit of salmon, tuna, and several varieties of bottom fish. The mouth of the Columbia here is considered one of the most treacherous bodies of water in the world and is aptly known as the "graveyard of the Pacific." Cape Disappointment has two lighthouses and is the home of the Coast Guard heavy-weather motor lifeboat station. In 1788 the English Captain John Meares, seeking the Columbia River, recorded missing the passage over the bar. In his discouragement he named the headland Cape Disappointment, and since then the treacherous waters have claimed some 230 boats. In fact, the *Oriole*, carrying materials for the first lighthouse, sank in 1853 while attempting its passage across the Columbia's infamous bar. The much-needed

Built on the considerable profits of the timber industry, Hoquiam Castle **right** is a fine example of turn-of-the-century architectural style.

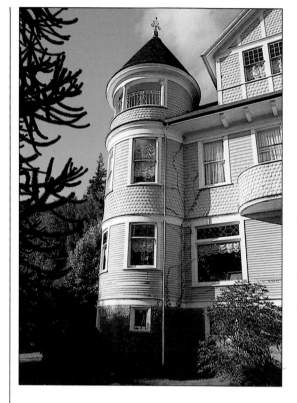

lighthouse did eventually get erected.

The town of Long Beach, just up from Ilwaco and Cape Disappointment, has long been the business center of the peninsula and offers surf-fishing as well as deep-sea fishing, swimming, and boating. Nearby, a research center operated by Washington State University explores the sex life of the cranberry. Known as the "Cape Cod" of the west coast, there are about 380 acres under cultivation on the peninsula. This is also a good place to hire a horse for an invigorating gallop along the board, flat beach.

Nahcotta, located on Willapa Bay, was named in honor of Chief Nahcati who first introduced the wonders of Willapa Bay to two white men, Mr. Clark and Mr. Espy. These two began harvesting oysters from the bay for shipment to San Francisco, establishing the town of Oysterville in 1854. Now a quiet, picturesque historical district, Oysterville was once a rip-roaring center of the oyster industry where saloon patronage outpulled church attendance figures on any given Sunday. When oyster schooners out of San Francisco arrived to pick up their cargo of these tiny bivalves, the oyster-bed owners

Seen here from the air, Washington's Long Beach peninsula **left** is a delightful step back in time. Broad, flat beaches run for miles, interrupted only by picture-postcard hamlets, cranberry bogs and the occasional inlet.

Fort Stevens **below** — originally built to ward off Confederate incursions up the Columbia during the Civil War—has the dubious distinction of being the only U.S. fort to have been fired on during World War II.

were paid in gold coin; at the high point of the industry, Oysterville's banks had more gold coin than any other town on the west coast (except, of course, San Francisco). For ballast the ships brought in building materials, and today there are some fine old homes dating from the 1860s and still standing, built of California redwood.

The spring migration is a good time to visit the Willapa National Wildlife Refuge where over 100 species of birds have been sighted, including whistling swans and Canadian geese. For shooting with a difference, Long Island, in the center of the bay, offers bow-and-arrow-hunting of deer, bear, and elk. Boat owners will delight in the strong summer northwest winds which, combined with the bay's protected waters, offer ideal conditions for catamarans or other shoal draft boats.

Returning to the mainland, at the northern tip of Willapa Bay, take a step back in time to visit the old towns of South Bend, Tokeland, and Raymond. Raymond is especially fascinating because it was originally elevated above the mud flats and the disintegrating wooden piles can still be traced. Nearby stands of timber fed 20 sawmills in what is now a sleepy

The placid waters of Lake Crescent **overleaf**, filling an ancient glacial trough, lie at the northernmost tip of Olympic National Park.

45

The inscrutable oyster built the town of Oysterville **above** on Willapa Bay at the northern end of the Long Beach peninsula. A rambunctious city in its late nineteenth-century heyday, Oysterville today is a sleepy near-ghost town.

An ocean setting and a temperate climate combine to make Victoria **below**, clustered on Vancouver Island's southern point, a city of constant delight.

village (with but two operating sawmills).

East of Raymond, between it and the Swiss-German village of Frances lies the body of young William Keil. For a really odd story it is worth the short detour inland to pay your respects at this unusual grave site. Young Willie had been promised a lead position in his parent's wagon train about to depart from Missouri. Unfortunately Willie died just before the train was scheduled to set out for the west. Dr. Keil, Willie's father, was the sort of man who kept his word. He immediately secured a lead-lined coffin, which he filled with alcohol to pickle his son's body. Willie's coffin was placed in the lead wagon as the train set off for the Oregon Territory. Bush telegraph purportedly alerted the Indians along the route that a dead man was leading this particular wagon train and, not wishing to mess with anyone's avenging spirits, the Indians gave the Keil party an uninterrupted and peaceful journey. Willie lies buried atop a hill near the village of Menlo.

Continuing north from Raymond is Grays Harbor. The American captain, Robert Gray, having set out in 1792 to search for the Northwest passage, discovered instead this great harbor, which is named for him. Then he and his party headed south and discovered the mouth of the Columbia River. The bog land around the harbor supports cranberries and an abundance of bird life. Hoquim's Castle, built in 1897 and situated on the mainland side of the harbor, is a study in nineteenth-century opulence and presumption. The town of Hoquim was built on lumbering profits and many of its turn-of-the-century buildings have been restored. Both Hoquim and nearby Aberdeen enjoyed considerably more rowdiness during the height of the timber trade when lumberjacks came to town to drink away their paychecks. Summer salmon-fishing and winter whale-watching are the featured activities now.

Washington's Olympic Peninsula,
beaches strewn with twisted piles of
driftwood, offers utter solitude
and a wilderness all its own.

Craigdarroch Castle **above right**, a truly stately home, betrays lavish nineteenth-century aspirations. Constructed by Scottish coal millionaire Robert Dunsmuir for his wife Joan, the Castle houses many fine works of art as well as period furnishings.

The twenty-mile-long stretch of beach running from Ocean Shores on the northern edge of the harbor to Moclips on the border of the Quinault Indian Reservation puts you firmly back into the twentieth century. Modern resorts offer gleaming service, and the broad, hard-packed beaches extending all along this stretch make for pleasant days spent playing by the ocean. Beachcombers can collect driftwood as well as all manner of jetsam and flotsam. Small restaurants along this coast feature local seafood—Dungeness crab, clams, oysters, salmon, rock, or bottom fish.

The coast route, SR 109, ends at the Quinault Indian Reservation, which borders on the Olympic National Forest—surely one of the better-sited federal reservations in the country. Surf-fishing and camping are featured on the reservation. On the eastern edge lies Lake Quinault fed by the Quinault River populated by some feisty steelhead.

A preponderance of national parks and forests in this northwestern corner of Washington ensures the protection of the area's wild beauty. A narrow 50-mile stretch of wilderness is preserved along the beach here as part of the Olympic National Park. Trails lead along deserted beaches and across incredibly beautiful headlands. Offshore, giant sea stacks rise from a sea that is nearly always turbulent. Winter visitors have a front-row seat for the storms that batter the coast. Rustic log cabins perched on cliff tops at Kalaloch just north of the Quinault Reservation provide cozy views of all the action.

At the northern edge of the Olympic National Park seaside strip is the Ozette Indian village archaeological site containing an unusually complete cultural record of the Makah Indian Nation. Referred to as a "Pompeii in Mud," the village was preserved over 500 years ago and is an anthropologist's dream. The Wedding Rock petroglyphs here are a fine example of primitive art, and wolf-claw carvings in the rock are a testimony to the now-extinct Olympic wolves that once roamed this coast.

North of Ozette is the Makah Indian Reservation, which enjoys a breathtaking position on the very tip of the peninsula, with Cape Flattery on its Pacific edge and the small town of Neah Bay just inside the Strait of Juan de Fuca.

Donated by British Columbians of Dutch heritage, the Centennial Bell Tower **left** houses over 60 bells. The tower is located in Heritage Court near the Provincial Museum and the Parliament buildings.

Declared a British Crown Colony in 1849 but controlled in practice by the Hudson's Bay Company, British Columbia knew no parliamentary government until 1856, when Victoria **left** became its administrative seat. The stately neo-Gothic Parliament buildings **below** were officially opened in 1898 and visitors may attend legislative sessions.

Viewing the buildings after dark **overleaf**, when they are picked out by a myriad of lights, lends an air of fantasy to the inner harbor. **51**

A pretty spot for a summer's day, Bastion Square **right** provides fine views over Victoria's busy harbor. The square, where James Douglas established Fort Victoria in 1843, is an appealing blend of old and new: restored buildings surrounded by fashionable restaurants and shops.

Once a brawling seaport and colonial headquarters, Victoria's inner harbor today provides a picturesque gateway to this very cosmopolitan city. The steamship *Princess Marguerite* **right** makes regular trips between Seattle and Victoria.

Vancouver Island

Vancouver Island, lying just north across the Strait of Juan de Fuca, presents British Columbia's attractions in a nutshell—if you go nowhere else in the province, Vancouver Island must claim part of your time. In fact, if you go nowhere else in the entire Pacific Northwest do NOT miss Vancouver Island. The warming current that flows here from across the Pacific keeps the island climate moderate, cool in winter, warm in summer. And, because it is an island, no point here is more than 40 miles from the sea, with the result that the population has more boats per person than in any other place in the world.

Credit for the discovery of Vancouver Island goes to Captain Cook, who landed at Nootka Sound on its western side in 1778. Spanish explorers were also in the vicinity about the same time, and as a result Spanish names intermingle happily with British place names along the island's coast. It was Captain George Vancouver who conducted much of the early exploration of the island and claimed it for Britain during the period 1791 to 1795—hence the name of the island today. The Hudson's Bay Company Fort Victoria, established in 1843, became the administrative headquarters of Victoria City in 1849.

Victoria

Nineteenth-century British fur traders forced north from the Oregon Territory by aggressive American trappers found a scenic, open land with an excellent harbor at the southern end of the island. The government of British Columbia is based here in the city of Victoria, and the magnificent stone Parliament buildings with the next-door Empress Hotel seem to personify the staid, colonial style of the late-nineteenth-century city. Victoria is the largest

One of the few open-air markets in the country **left**, Pike Place Market in Seattle is also one of the few remaining farmers' marts where fresh produce and seafood abound.

Turn-of-the-century "Oriental" architecture such as the Chinese school **below** provides a visual feast for visitors to Victoria's Chinatown.

Long stretches of desolate sand
dominate the scenery from Sooke to Port
Renfrew, north of Victoria.

Fort Rodd, a few miles west
of Victoria, served as a coastal artillery
installation during the late
nineteenth century. The lighthouse still
guards the entrance to Esquimault
Harbor. Directly across from Fort Rodd lie the
naval dockyards featuring one
of the world's largest dry-docks.

The stately Empress Hotel **center**, first opened in 1908, typifies the city's British flavor with its daily ritual of high tea,

city on the island, and its cosmopolitan makeup reflects the immigration pattern that helped to establish it. At the north end of town is British Columbia's oldest Chinatown, started in the gold rush of the late 1850s, with its magnificent Gate of Harmonious Interest marking the entrance.

Near Victoria

North of Victoria is the Saanich Peninsula, which features winding rural back roads, some

The cultural diversity of Victoria is one of its great attractions. Chinatown, at the north end of old town, is British Columbia's oldest, with the Gate of Harmonious Interest **right** marking its entrance. Mouth-watering aromas of dim sum and black-bean crab tempt the hungry visitor.

freshwater fishing lakes, and the world-famous Butchart Gardens. The horticultural displays change with the seasons in these gardens. From the northern tip of this peninsula ferries depart for the mainland, Gulf Islands, and Washington State.

To the west of Victoria, from Sooke to Port Renfrew the scenery becomes wilder and rain forests begin to dominate. (Indeed, the absence of roads on the western side of the island testifies to the difficult, rugged terrain.) Best-known of the beaches here are French and China, with long stretches of empty sand, and Botanical, with its rocky tidal pools. Port Renfrew, at the end of the public road, is the gateway to the logging districts that crisscross the islands; it is also the beginning of the West Coast Trail, the island's 72-kilometer coastal

Sea lions **above** gather on the Broken Islands off Vancouver Island's west coast. Coming to rockeries such as this to bear their young, the animals group into hotly contested harems consisting of one bull and several cows. While the cows nurse, the bulls engage in fierce contests to protect their domain.

Flotillas of ferry boats glide gracefully in and out of Vancouver Island's many harbors. This shows Swartz Bay **left** on the Saanich Peninsula, north of Victoria.

Victoria is eminently British
in atmosphere, and one thing the British and
their colonial offspring do well
is garden. From the delicate Japanese garden
left, to the exquisite English
rose garden **above**, the 35-acre Butchart
Gardens makes up one of the
Pacific Northwest's most picturesque corners.
Begun in 1904 on a worked-out
quarry on the Butchart estate, these gardens
began as a personal hobby and
soon became a commitment to horticulture.

'Endless' and 'wild' describe the coastline running from Long Beach **top left**.

On the beach at Carmanah Head, hikers **center** stride out toward the lighthouse on the West Coast Trail, Vancouver Island's 44-mile coastal hiking challenge. The trail, which averages six days' walking, meanders from Port Renfrew to Bamfield.

An angler tries his luck **right** in the placid Cowichan River. At other points along the river its twists and whitewater attract kayakers and canoeists.

Previous page Lying on the eastern edge of the Quinault Indian Reservation, Lake Quinault is home to several species of game fish, including the famous fighting steelhead. Here a long Quinault fisherman enjoys the sunset.

hiking challenge. The trail crosses over plunging ravines and traverses along coastal bluffs and deep into forests, calling on skills that include stamina and strength. The average length of time to hike the trail, originating in Port Renfrew and finishing at Bamfield, is six days.

Victoria, **centre**, is certainly Canada's most beautiful capital city. Its mild climate, combined with a relaxed pace and spectacular natural setting make it a truly "liveable" city.

Northern Vancouver Island

The Trans-Canada Highway leads north from Victoria, a spectacular drive (or bicycle ride) along the rock walls that rise above Finlayson Arm and Mill Bay. The first important stop (if you don't count the country pubs along the road) is the little town of Goldstream—the site of one of the best salmon runs in the province. During late October, it is possible to watch the amorous salmon's upstream struggle along the river. Nearby, on the salt flats, migrating swans, geese, and ducks gather for a different kind of mating dance. The Malahat summit behind Goldstream has the best view of the Gulf Islands. These islands, which you can reach by ferry, are quiet retreats snuggled close to the main island, yet still far enough away, ranging in size from a few rocks poking out of the sea to the largest, Saltspring, with its own mountain and lake.

From the Malahat summit, the highway descends into the Cowichan valley, a pleasant agricultural and logging area. The coastal plain between sea and mountains is at its widest here. On the east side of the plane is Cowichan Bay, offering excellent fishing and fresh seafood chowders in its several tiny restaurants. To the west of the town of Duncan lies Cowichan Lake, a long narrow stretch of water reaching into the island's mountain spine. Fishing, boating, and waterskiing are the focus of activities here. A wildflower reserve carpets the forest floor at Honeymoon Bay near the lake, and the Cowichan River challenges intrepid kayakers and canoeists. The Cowichan is also the site of an annual kayak slalom competition every summer.

It is a mistake to hurry north and bypass the small seaside communities of Maple Bay, Crof-

The whistle of a steam train sounds as the locomotive **above** rounds a bend in the specially constructed track. The British Columbia Forest Museum, home of the train, also features logging equipment as well as other steam locomotives from the early days.

Stretching north of Victoria, the Saanich Peninsula **right** features Elk Lake and Beaver Lake, perfect spots for windsurfing. Ferries leave from Tod Inlet and run across to the mainland at Mill Bay.

ton, and Chemainus—the last a once thriving mill town now resuscitated as a picturesque village. The town's buildings are adorned with larger-than-life murals of its history.

North of Chemainus lies the company town of Ladysmith, placed exactly on the 49th parallel—the Canadian–U.S. border for mainland British Columbia. When the surrounding coal mines encouraged a sharp population increase in the early part of this century, Ladysmith was founded as a healthy escape from the grime of the mines.

To the west of Ladysmith is the Green Mountain ski area, the Nanaimo Lakes chain, and the old villages and slag heaps that bear testimony to King Coal. Seaside resorts, notably Yellowpoint, lie along the eastern coast, and the Cedar road passes through lovely farmland with the requisite country pubs.

North of Ladysmith is Nanaimo. This town enjoys something more than a reputation as a commercial center for it is also the home of the World Championship Bathtub Race, held every year across the Georgia Strait from Nanaimo to Vancouver city. This race attracts competitors from as far away as Australia—and the Aussies have had the temerity to win this race for several years in a row, much to the consternation of the island competitors. Apart from the hilarity of the bathtub race Nanaimo also offers arts, and its theatre is home to an excellent professional Shakespeare Festival.

North of Nanaimo are the beaches at Parksville and Qualicum, which together provide a huge stretch of sand, prime areas for beachcombing, kite-flying, or castle construction. In fact, the annual Parksville sandcastle-building contest sees four-story edifices and other architectural wonders being constructed during the July competition. Parksville is also the home of the World Croquet Championships, played every August, and it need hardly be said that the contestants do indeed take this competition dead seriously. If golf is your game, Parksville offers year-round play on greens and tees providing panoramic views out over the Strait of Georgia to the coastal mountains on the mainland. And if you're not already sick to death of salmon the Qualicum area is a good base for fishing expeditions.

The Hudson's Bay Company
Fort Bastion, at Nanaimo, is a reminder of the
near-autocractic power the
fur-trapping outfit once held over British
Columbia in general and Vancouver
Island in particular.

Nanaimo **above**, on the east side of Vancouver Island, is home to a thriving arts colony and a professional Shakespeare Festival.

With its rocky tidal pools and abundant intertidal life, Botanical Beach **middle** is a living laboratory for amateur biologists.

Picturesque, yes—but necessary too: lofty lighthouses, like this one on Vancouver Island's western edge **below**, punctuate the Pacific Northwest coast.

The Vancouver Coastline

Although the flow of the island tends to be south-north, there are several major roads cutting west across the mountains and one of these leads from Parksville up over the mountains and down into the Alberni valley. En route is Mount Arrowsmith, a haven for skiers and hikers. Port Alberni, sitting at the head of the long inlet reaching in from the Pacific Ocean on the west side of the island, began life as a mill town. Today its protected waters are acknowledged as one of the best spots for salmon-fishing in the province. Numerous lakes around the town, such as Sproat and Great Central, also offer freshwater fishing and recreation. Orcas—killer whales—are known to inhabit these waters, and visitors can take the sturdy MV *Lady Rose* down the inlet to its mouth where whales can some-

A lone ferryboat **previous page** plies the beautiful waters off Cowichan Bay, Vancouver Island.

times be seen cavorting offshore from the tiny towns of Ucluelet and Bamfield. Bamfield, a logging and fishing town, is also the northern end of the West Coast Trail.

The Broken Islands lie offshore at the entrance to Barkley Sound and provide excellent viewpoints (by boat) for watching sea lions, seals, and migrating gray whales. Really intrepid canoeists and kayakers can ply the (relatively) protected waters of the channel between the islands.

For an unmatched view of wild coastline take the road from Port Alberni to Tofino and the Pacific Rim National Park. It may be difficult to believe, as you watch the moody ocean crush against the shore, but Spanish explorer Balboa found this sea so mild and quiet in 1513 tha he named it the "Pacific Ocean." Bear in mind that Vancouver Island's west coast has been dubbed the "graveyard of the Pacific." The ships that lie at the bottom here furnish excellent opportunities for scuba divers and also provide haven to hundreds of different kinds of fish. Then, if you get too cold, you can always relax into Hot Springs Cove, accessible

Painter's Lodge **above** on the legendary Campbell River, north of Courtenay, holds special significance for sport fishermen: for years the Campbell and salmon fishing have been synonymous.

There are still some fine old traditions in this hi-tech age. The World Championship Bathtub Race **middle**, held annually across the Georgia Strait to Vancouver city, gets its official start courtesy of the mayor of Nanaimo.

One of Vancouver Island's premier ski areas is Mount Arrowsmith **below**. Hikers frequent the same slopes when the snow melts.

Parksville **above** hosts two competitive and serious events: July sees a sandcastle-building event followed by the World Croquet Championships in August.

Scattered between Puget Sound and Canadian waters, the 172 islands of the San Juan group **below** offer tranquil charm.

by boat or float plane just north of Tofino, with the rain forest at your back and a view of the Pacific at your feet.

Is there a serious fisherman who has not heard of the legendary Campbell River, north of Courtenay? Salmon-fishing and the name of this town have been linked for years, and it is also home to the Tyee Club. Membership in this exclusive fraternity goes only to those fortunate few who have caught a tyee salmon weighing more than 30 pounds—from a row-boat—on light tackle—in one of two local pools.

While earliest white settlers did their best to decimate Indian culture, nearby Quadra Island is home to the shell-shaped Kwakiutl Museum at Cape Mudge. Both the museum and the several totem poles standing outside give the visitor a chance to understand past and present Indian life-styles.

From Campbell River a major road leads west over the mountains to the inlets on the western edge of the island. En route is Strath-cona Provincial Park—the province's oldest park and the island's largest wilderness area. Numerous hiking trails there encompass all grades of difficulty from leisurely walks to test-ing terrain. West of the park is the tiny town of Gold River, landing site of Captain Cook when he was busy claiming everything in sight for the British. Today Nootka Cove and the surrounding country have gone back to the original native inhabitants, and the motor vessel *Uchuck* (which you might do if the seas are rough) is the only link between these isolated logging and fishing camps.

The northern third of Vancouver Island, the area around Port McNeill, Alert Bay, and Port Hardy, offers wilderness where fishing and hiking opportunities abound. Alert Bay, on an island just off the coast, has a fascinating Indian cemetery and some of the best totem poles still standing in natural settings. Some of the earliest settlers to this area came to estab-lish Utopia—Finnish settlers founded Sointula on Malcolm Island and Danish emigrants founded Holberg on the west coast. Although neither group created the ideal, both com-munities were long-lasting and are still vibrant today.

Whaling was an early industry in the area and whales can still be seen here, especially in Robson Bight and Johnstone Strait. Whale-watching expeditions leave from Telegraph

Brilliant cascades of water tumble down Englishman Falls **left**. Just inland from Qualicum beach, Indian petroglyphs can also be seen along the river.

The **totem pole** was used by Indians to symbolize the spirit of past generations. Carved on it were representations of human ancestors and animals, plants and birds. Indians believed that every animal and plant had its own particular power which it could exert on other creatures.

Dorsal fins of a group of orcas (killer whales) **overleaf** slice silently through the chilly waters off Vancouver Island. With distinctive black-and-white markings, an orca has such a fine hydrodynamic shape that it can bring its head nearly three-quarters out of the water before it breaks the surface.

Sandcastle construction **above** is a serious endeavor on Parksville beach. Together with Qualicum beach, this coastal area provides a huge stretch of sand.

One of the more awe-inspiring behaviors in the whale's considerable repertory is "spyhopping" **middle**. Theories for this action abound: play, visual-orientation or simply "getting the lay of the land" for navigational purposes.

Hardy sunbathers **below** enjoy the beach at Qualicum, north of Nanaimo. At low tide the beaches stretch well out into the ocean, providing a huge playground of sand and tidepools.

Found in the forest, where they feed on berries, honey, insects and small mammals, **grizzly bears** can grow to a height of more than eight feet.

Cove, a village on stilts fronted by a long wooden boardwalk.

Not so lucky as the Scandinavian immigrants near Alert Bay, other intrepid settlers attempted to build their homesteads on Cape Scott on the very northwestern tip of the big island. Between the winter storms and the summer fogs (and, one suspects, the isolation) these settlers were defeated. Today their abandoned homes form a sort of ghost colony, enclosed within the boundaries of Scott Provincial Park. Trails to the tip of Cape Scott and to San Josef Bay wind through rain forests to deserted beaches facing the open Pacific.

The Inside Passage

Port Hardy, at the end of the paved road, is a fishing, logging, and mining center. It is also a stop on the run north through the Inside Passage from Victoria to Prince Rupert. A trip absolutely unlike any other, for almost 275 miles you never lose sight of land and the scenery along the way is nothing short of spectacular. The heavily forested shores are home to a multitude of animal life including eagles, bears, and elk, which can often be seen on the shore. Fjords, coastal glaciers, and rocky islets are similarly the hauling-out places for seals, sea lions, and all manner of birds. The seas in this area are sometimes crowded with marine life from killer whales to the occasional Beluga (white) whales. The ferry also stops once a week for 30 minutes at Bella Bella, midway up the coast. It was at this small village, then as now inhabited mostly by Indians, that the first white man to make the overland traverse across Canada, Alexander Mackenzie, finished his journey. And at Prince Rupert, visitors can see totem poles still standing throughout the port.

Hiking along Barkley Sound
is a good way to observe seals, sea lions and
migrating gray whales.
Brave-hearted canoeists and kayakers also
make their way through these
frigid waters.

Vancouver City

Across the Strait of Georgia from Victoria is the city of Vancouver, the gem of mainland British Columbia. Fully three-quarters of the province's total population reside in and around this cosmopolitan city, which backs up to the mountains and faces the water. Its port is Canada's gateway to the Orient, a fact reflected in its exotic makeup. Its museums and parks are a tourist mecca, and its recreation facilities help ease the tension of city-living for residents and visitors alike. In Vancouver it is possible to be in heaven without first dying— in this beautiful city you can ski in the morning and sail in the afternoon.

While Captain George Vancouver was busy charting Vancouver Island he also took time to row across the strait, through the narrow Burrard Inlet, and into the lovely, sheltered harbor. Staying just long enough to name the

Good mountaineering, where 'brave' rubs shoulders with 'foolish', demands special skills, not least of which is knowing when not to climb. These two **opposite** ascending a crag at Strathcona Provincial Park demonstrate safe techniques.

Travelers to the remote northern tip of Vancouver Island are rewarded with a step back into history at Alert Bay **above**. On an island just off the coast the U'Mista Culture Museum records ancient Indian culture.

Precipitous cascades at Della Falls **middle** carve future crags. The park is the oldest in the province.

The end of the Inside Passage, Prince Rupert **below** is still much as it was when the first British trappers arrived during the eighteenth century.

Overleaf, the sweeping skyline of Vancouver—a cosmopolitan blend of almost three-quarters of the total population of British Columbia.

The skeleton of an abandoned
wharf bears lonely witness to the demise of
an utopian dream on the
very northwestern tip of Vancouver Island.
Cape Scott Provincial Park
marks the area where a group of Scandinavian
emigrants attempted, and
failed, to homestead.

A ferry glides through the fjord-like
scenery of the Inside Passage running from
Victoria north to Prince Rupert.

Vertigo-sufferers should avoid the Capilano Suspension Bridge, **right**, 230 shaky feet above the water. In 1899 the spot quickly became a popular destination for day-outings from the city of Vancouver when a lodge and bridge were constructed here. The bridge sways ever so gently.

Coming in for a graceful landing, osprey such as this **far left** are part of the multitude of animal life to be seen along the heavily forested shores of the Inside Passage.

A solitary fishing boat **left** heads out to sea at Bella Coola. The hospitable Indians of this area welcomed Alexander Mackenzie, the first white man to arrive in their midst, in 1793.

Stanley Park, Vancouver, **below** is a fir and pine filled paradise in the middle of a modern and bustling city.

place for himself, he turned around and set sail for England the very next day, and the region returned to its peaceful backwater existence. The fur-trapping companies of Britain held this country exclusively from around the beginning of the nineteenth century until 1858, when gold was discovered on the Fraser River. The combined factors of gold fever and the completion of the railroad to Vancouver in 1887 helped to increase the city's population, which by the turn of the century had explored to over 100,000 souls. Vancouver today is a city of little Vancouvers as a result—Italian, Chinese, Ukranian, East Indian, Filipino—but it is overlaid with British overtones. Festivities accordingly encompass everything from the Chinese New Year's Parade to cricket matches and the "Polar Bear Swim" across English Bay on New Year's Day (only the products of English public schools could dream up such "fun").

The sites to see in Vancouver are legion, from the Capilano Suspension Bridge (not for the fainthearted) to the "World's Thinnest Office Building" (according to Ripley's "Believe it or not"), on the corner of Pender and Carrall streets. The University of British Columbia has an excellent Museum of Anthropology, and the Vancouver Public Aquarium has marine denizens that include killer and Beluga whales, dolphins, and other birds and mammals of the sea. The city has multitudes of greenery-laced parks, excellent art galleries, and restaurants catering to all tastes.

The mysterious symbolism of totem poles **above** attracts a visitor's attention at a park overlooking the harbor at Prince Rupert.

Totem Poles

The Indians of Vancouver Island, as elsewhere in the Pacific Northwest, created many fine examples of pictorial art **right**. Presented as part of a display in a park near the center of Victoria, these totem poles now represent a vanishing art.

Indians of the west coast had access to so much wealth which was so easily obtainable that they also possessed a commodity unheard of in the eighteenth and nineteenth centuries: leisure time. With this leisure time they developed a talent for carving and pictorial art, creating many designs that have come down to us today, notably the tall totem poles still to be found occasionally in the woods and museums of the Pacific Northwest.

If you accept the anthropologists' theory that totemism is the association of an animal or plant with a human clan, then a totem pole becomes a kind of visual *Roots*—a visual genealogy. The totem pole's various birds or animals represent the tribe's ancestors and their attributes or abilities—for example, the eagle's keen eyesight or the bear's brave ferocity. Although local myths and legends unique to one tribe were reflected in the different details of the poles, the figures usually had the same principle characteristics: a grizzly bear clutching a shield, a beaver with a cross-hatched tail and enormous teeth. Many of the poles to be seen today are topped with the mythical thunderbird, lightning flashing from its eyes, that symbolized the Great Spirit. Other common animal symbols were the raven with large wings and a long beak, the eagle with its sharply curved beak, the killer whale, the frog, and the shark.

Totem poles probably originally functioned as roof supports for the wooden houses the coastal Indians built in their villages. These roof supports became more decorative, without losing their function, when the animal figure at the base of the pole had a mouth large enough to serve as an entrance to the house. Very elaborate poles were erected to stand alone outside a chief's house as a symbol of his authority and importance. Funeral poles were erected beside a grave. All poles were elaborate and, to our eyes, mysterious. The symbolic animal representations are usually easily recognized by certain prominent

Indians of the Gitksan tribe **left** model elaborately worked ceremonial blankets in a longhouse—one of seven tribal houses at the 'Ksan village near Hazelton, B.C. The village, a rich showplace of Indian culture, also has authentic totem poles on display.

features, such as the flat tail of the beaver, but just exactly what the beaver symbolized for a particular tribal clan is unknown to us.

You can see totem poles today in many museums and parks throughout the Pacific Northwest. The Provincial Museum in Victoria and the recreated 'Ksan village near Hazelton, B.C., both have authentic totem poles on display. Or you can view the world's tallest totem pole at the U'Mista Museum, Alert Bay on Cormorant Island, B.C.—all 54 meters of it! Pioneer Square in Seattle, Washington, has a huge totem pole, also reputed to be one of the world's tallest. To see the totem poles in authentic settings, but usually in varying stages of decay, visit one of the many Indian villages in the Queen Charlotte Islands, B.C. (such a visit usually requires governmental permission beforehand), or explore along Lake Quinault on the Olympic Peninsula, Washington. At the Museum of Northern British Columbia in Prince Rupert you can watch Indian artists at work in the totem-pole-carving shed. In Anacortes, Washington, you can watch totem poles being carved and even purchase one to take home—if your garden is large enough!

Totemism **left** is the association of an animal's characteristics with a human clan—a kind of visual *Roots*. For example: the eagle's keen eyesight is represented at the top of this small totem while the bear's ferocity is portrayed at the bottom.

British Columbia's Provincial Museum in Victoria is a must for visitors wanting to see some of the Pacific Northwest's finest remaining totem poles. Experts believe that totem poles originally functioned as simple roof supports for the coastal Indians' wooden houses. Totem poles quickly evolved into more elaborate creations that were adopted by chiefs to symbolize their authority. They served as funeral poles and eventually stood alone as watchful sentinels for the entire tribe. Representing various attributes of a human clan, totems were often topped by the mythical thunderbird that symbolized the Great Spirit **right**.

OREGON'S WESTERN RIVER VALLEYS

Even after the coming of the railway, the **covered wagon** remained a familiar sight, as families moved west in search of virgin soil.

Opposite One of the few paved roads piercing Olympic National Park, the "Heart o' the Hills" route leads up to the alpine pastures of Hurricane Ridge, offering fine views over the jagged peaks in the interior of the park.

When the great immigrant tide began streaming across the Oregon Trail in the middle of the nineteenth century, they were mostly heading for the hospitable western river valleys of Oregon: the Willamette valley in the north and the Umpqua and Rogue River valleys to the south. These valleys, nestled between the Coast Mountains and the Cascade Range, beckoned the early settlers with fertile, sheltered farmland. From a tiny, isolated population of 200 in 1840 (not including trappers or Indians), the white population mushroomed within five years to 3,000 souls.

Although the wetness of the climate sometimes weighed heavily on the immigrant's optimism—one woman confided to her diary, "I cannot tell you how gloomy it is here"—it also created an evergreen valley. The rich, alluvial topsoil, deposited by hundreds of streams and rivers, combined with a mild (although assuredly wet) climate to produce an abundance of thriving crops.

It was trappers from the Hudson's Bay Company that arrived here first in the early nineteenth century, pursuing the hapless beaver for its valuable pelt. When a few French-Canadians decided to give up the fur-trade and settle as farmers, the value of the region for agriculture quickly became apparent. But in 1833, an extraordinary plea was received from a party of four Indians—a plea that would alter the course of American history. Arriving in Saint Louis after traveling overland across the Rockies, this group—three Nez Percés and one Flathead—announced that their people wanted to learn the source of the white man's power, specifically the contents of a great book which they believed detailed the white man's "true" way of worshipping the Great Spirit. When, for added pathos, two of the Indians promptly dropped dead of exhaustion, the missionary societies were electrified: to bring civilization and Christianity to the dark savages, *at their own request*. Two Methodist ministers, Jason and Daniel Lee, promptly set out for the Oregon country in 1834. Finding the Willamette valley's soil rich and welcoming the Lees spread the word via letters to their mission board back in the United States. A wagon-train migration began in earnest almost immediately. The Indian population quickly learned not only the source of the white man's power, but also the white man's seemingly insatiable lust for land as Indian pastures and hunting grounds were fenced and plowed. In very short order the Indians were excluded from the valley by the sheer force of white immigration.

Hill Country

The southern end of Oregon's western river valley is characterized by rolling hills landscaped with tidy farms that give way to stands of timber at higher elevations. Physical laziness can be your only limit to the abundance of recreational pursuits here. This part of the valley nestles against the Cascades on its eastern edge and is backed up along the border with California by the Siskiyou Mountains; two wild river systems, the Umpqua and Rogue, flow unobstructed to the Pacific from their starting points high on the western slopes of the Cascades.

Interstate Highway 5 is the major artery running through this valley from Ashland in the south to Portland on the Washington-Oregon border. Once known as the Oregon-California Trail, it was the major route for stagecoaches linking Portland and Sacramento. The danger of bandits swooping down out of the hills meant that the stage drivers and their outriders had to be a fairly tough bunch. Legend has it that one of the toughest and one of the meanest was "One-Eyed" Charlie Parkhurst—discovered to be Miss Charlotte Parkhurst after she died.

At the very southern end of the Rogue River valley, near the Oregon-California border, is the city of Ashland. Bringing culture to the green foothills of the Siskiyou Mountains, Ashland is a charming city famous for its Shakespearean Festival. Recipient of a 1983 Tony Award for "outstanding achievement in regional theatre" the festival has three theatres: from late February through October the Black Swan and the Angus Bowmer offer indoor plays; from June through September theatergoers can sit under the stars at the out-

West of Ashland in the Siskiyou Mountains is Oregon's Caves National Monument **right**, a fascinating subterranean world of wierdly shaped stalactites, marble pillars and streaks of pale limestone.

door Elizabethan Stagehouse to see plays presented as in Shakespeare's day, with sparse scenery but elegant costuming.

A short detour west off I-5 as you drive north takes you to Jacksonville. Jacksonville was in the heart of Oregon's first gold-strike country, and this entire town is protected as a national historic district with many buildings from the 1850s gold-mining boom era still standing. If you are near Jacksonville in August the Peter Britt Music Festival is international in scope and performs on the stately grounds of the old Peter Britt estate. As a counterpoint there is also an excellent, foot-stomping bluegrass festival held during the summer.

East of Jacksonville, back on I-5, is Medford, the commercial center of the Rogue River valley. Bear Creek, a tributary of the Upper Rogue River, winds through the center of town, and pear orchards and foothills surround Medford itself, creating a lovely vista. The city holds its salute to the fruit industry in April with the traditional Pear Blossom Festival, one of the several flower festivals held in Oregon annually. Among other events is the twelve-kilometer run—you know you're getting close to Oregon's running territory. And for an unusual trip you might try a moonlight float trip (with a guide!) on the Upper Rogue starting in Shady Cove, just northeast of Medford on Highway 62. Lost Creek Dam, north of Medford, has the state's largest fish hatchery. Needless to say, Lost Creek Reservoir behind the dam is exceptionally well stocked for fishing. The Rogue River National Forest is easily reached from the city via State Highway 62, giving access both to Crater Lake and to the final link in the Oregon Cascades' chain: 9,495-foot Mount McLoughlin.

From Medford I-5 jogs west to the two towns of Grants Pass and Rogue River, at the midpoint of the wild and scenic Rogue River's dash to the Pacific. Both towns serve as headquarters for the licensed guides and outfitters operating fishing and boat trips along the Rogue. The 40-mile Rogue River hiking trail has so many breathtaking overlooks you tend to become indifferent to "yet more" thrilling white-water rapids. The Memorial Day weekend is the official start of summer on the river, and Grants Pass celebrates with a festival featuring, among other events, a 35-mile

white-water race. But for a contest to write home about, go to the small town of Rogue River, just east of Grants Pass, for its splendid slice of American life: a rooster-crowing contest held every June.

Continuing north along I-5 the road descends out of the foothills to the (relatively) flat valley floor. If you should espy an elephant or lion just north of Winston, don't panic. This 600-acre Wildlife Safari reserve cages the humans and allows the animals to roam free. It is a nonprofit reserve, world famous for its programs to breed cheetah's—a shy, elusive endangered animal, exceedingly difficult to breed. The reserve offers interpretative programs as well as the chance to feed and pet some of these beautiful African creatures.

Roseburg is situated on the east bank of the South Umpqua River. Just a few minutes away is the North Umpqua with its deep, clear pools and excellent fly-fishing opportunities for anyone intent on casting for steelhead and rainbow trout. If you'd rather watch than catch, Winchester Dam is a good spot to see migrating salmon and steelhead climbing the fish ladders in their annual "drive" home. Hiking trails along the main river and its tributaries lead to fascinating rock formations and waterfalls. Rosenburg itself was a timber area, and the city's Douglas County Museum houses logging equipment and interpretative information. The museum also has information on the area's covered bridges and Victorian-era homes—notably the residence of Oregon's first territorial governor, General Joseph Lane.

The **Oregon white oak**, the only species of oak tree found in Washington and British Columbia, has sweet, edible acorns.

The Willamette Valley

The Willamette valley, beginning near the small town of Cottage Grove, has Oregon's finest soil and the bulk of the state's population. The valley's cities include the capital, Salem, as well as several of the oldest communities in the west. Farmers tend luxuriant crops including wheat, berries,and nuts; most of the state's wineries are located along this valley as well. In addition to the Willamette River there are plenty of other streams, lakes,

The waters of Lake Crescent **overleaf**, a popular resort area on the Olympic Peninsula, brood silently as night falls.

Looking east from the headwaters of the Metolius River, the snow-clad dome of Mount Jefferson **right** sparkles in the bright sunshine.

Quiet, prosperous farms **center**, fed by the Columbia and its tributaries, landscape Bradley and the rural valleys of Oregon.

and reservoirs as well as stunning mountain peaks beckoning hikers, climbers, skiers, and photographers. Cottage Grove, at the very southern fringe of the valley, is the gateway to the gold-mining heritage in the hills southeast of town. Visitors should ask for information on the scenic loop drive through the old mining district and its cluster of covered bridges (and occasional ghost town's).

The town of Oakridge, northeast of Cottage Grove on SR 58, is surrounded by the recreational wealth of the Willamette National Forest. You can sail, water ski, or fish on Waldo Lake in the summer and ski at the Willamette Pass Ski Area in the winter. Three major peaks tower above this region, dominated by 10,495-foot Mount Jefferson, surrounded by the federal wilderness area of the same name. Three-Fingered Jack and Mount Washington break the skyline, offering climbing challenges to the brave.

Any self-respecting track and field fan will know that Eugene is the "Race Capital of the World." The city and its university regularly host top national and regional meets. A July Fourth event with the delightful title "Butte to

Butte" attracts world-class athletes. In addition to the city's numerous running paths (try the Prefontaine Trail), bicycle trails along the Willamette River are also popular.

North of Eugene is the little town of Junction City, which celebrates its Scandinavian heritage in mid-August. The festival is a four-day event in our egalitarian country, with each dedicated to one of the four Nordic countries—Norway, Sweden, Finland, and Denmark.

Continuing north along I-5, take US 20 west to Corvallis. "Corvallis" is roughly translated as "heart of the valley" which it is geographically, and, because of its location it served as the territorial capital and shipping center. Although no longer the capital it is worth a visit for its formal rose and rhododendron gardens, two hallmarks of the Pacific Northwest. The William L. Finley National Wildlife Refuge is a good place to spot rarely seen birds. Philomath, just six miles from Corvallis, is the recreation gateway to the Coast Range.

Returning to I-5, Albany is an old town with an impressive array of Victorian-era buildings and a Fourth of July event that shouldn't be missed unless you're on your death bed. The World Championships Timber Carnival draws brawny lumberjacks from all over to Albany in order to compete in such events as axe throwing, log rolling, and tree topping.

The area west of Albany served by US 20 and a number of small county roads is well worth a few days' detour. The village of Scio, east of Albany, is in the center of the region's covered-bridge cluster. Scio also hosts the Northwest Championship Sheep Dog Trials in

With its towering Sitka spruce, Western hemlock, Douglas fir and Western cedar awash in spongy moss and dense undergrowth, the Hoh valley **left** seems the epitome of a primordial rain forest.

late May—a fascinating exhibition of the finely tuned communication possible between a man standing stationary in a field and his faithful dog responding to whistles alone. Also nearby is Lebanon, famous for its June Strawberry Festival, featuring the world's largest diet-breaker: a strawberry shortcake weighing in at more than 6,000 pounds.

Oregon's state capital, Salem, is just an hour south from Portland with the beaches a short distance to the west and the Cascades even closer to the east. The 121 steps leading to the capitol tower give a good view of all these possibilities. At Bush's Pasture Park you can tour Bush House—a large nineteenth-century home—and stroll through both a formal rose garden and a less structured wildflower garden. The missionary Jason Lee founded Willamette University herb in 1842—the oldest university west of the Rockies. East of Salem, along SR 22, are Mill City and Gates, supply centers for white-water adventures on the North Santiam River.

It is worth your time to take a step back in time, get off the interstate, and explore some of the rural roads northeast of Salem, principally along Highway 99E. The sizable German-Swiss population of Mount Angel holds a boistrous "Oktoberfest" every September when you can make a glutton of yourself on traditional sausages, smoked meats, homemade cheese, and cole slaw—all washed down with an abundance of beer. For a view of this lovely countryside drive up to Mount Angel Abbey. Once a place of worship for the local Indian population, this 330-foot butte is now the location of a Benedictine monastery estab-

lished by Swiss monks. The abbey's strikingly modern library was designed by noted Finnish architect Alvar Aalto. Northeast of Mount Angel, Molalla also holds a Fourth of July "Buckeroo" rodeo featuring the Northwest's top cowboys, while neighboring Brooks hosts a fair featuring antique steam-powered farm equipment; Woodburn is the improbable site of a Mexican fiesta in early August. Aurora, similar to Mount Angel, was established as a religious communal colony in the nineteenth century and today is designated a national historic landmark district.

Equally old and picturesque is the area northwest of Salem, notably the three small towns of McMinnville, Newburg, and Saint Paul. Here clusters of several of Oregon's wineries and the nut industry are based—specifically hazelnuts, officially known as "filberts." The town of Saint Paul has a Fourth of July rodeo, billed as the largest in the Pacific Northwest. But if you really want to be entertained—and if you always harbored secret doubts about the intelligence of turkeys—run, don't walk, to the McMinnville Turkey-Rama held from July 12 to 14. A festival honoring the

Not for the faint-hearted, this.
Two contestants demonstrate their
speed-climbing bravado in the
pole-climb—one of the many events in
Albany's annual World
Championship Timber Carnival.

Willamette valley's turkey industry, the festivities climax with a turkey race that will have you clutching your sides and gasping for air. West of McMinnville is the historic village of Newbury with its many old homes, including the boyhood home of Herbert Hoover.

Portland

If a pioneer from Maine hadn't won the toss of a coin in 1845, Oregon's largest city and port would have been named Boston. Thus were the momentous decisions of our past made by our revered forefathers. Portland's strategic location has long made it one of the Pacific Northwest's major export centers. Starting out life as a supply port to the California gold fields, Portland blossomed quickly because of the increased steamboat traffic on the Willamette and the Columbia.

Despite its continuing commercial importance the city's natural beauty has not been tarnished. The City of Roses is indeed a lovely city of fountains, gardens, and parks with a quality of life—so its citizens claim—unequaled anywhere else on earth. That claim may hold true if you care for winter sports (Mount Hood), are not indifferent to river float trips (Willamette and the Columbia) or can get excited by spectacular scenery (Columbia River Gorge)—all within a half-hour's drive from Portland. In fact, with its more than 160 parks and numerous fountains you needn't even venture outside downtown to feel the cool relief of green open space. And the City of Roses lives up to its name from mid-May until late November when over 10,000 rose bushes of 400 varieties blossom in the city's International Rose Test Gardens. Just to perfect the photographer's dream, on clear days the snow-capped peak of 11,235-foot Mount Hood forms a spectacular backdrop behind the rose gardens. 5,000 acres of greenbelt containing 30 miles of hiking and biking trails within the city limits can keep even the most hyperactive hiker in shape. And if the majesty of Mother Nature hasn't so far impressed you, Mount St.

Helens is visible to the north, across the Columbia, when it's puffing steam.

The Chehalis Valley

Continuing north from Portland, across the lower Columbia and the state line is the southwest section of Washington. This area, just inland from Washington's coast, is comprised of the agricultural Chehalis valley along the lower Columbia, culminating in the Olympic Peninsula in the extreme northwest corner of the state. The lower portion of the valley is a prosperous countryside, reminiscent of Europe with its neatly laid-out farms and well-fed livestock. As you continue north, passing through the state capital at Olympia, the valley ends at the southern reaches of Puget Sound. From here a slight jog west takes you to the edge of the sparsely populated and virtually roadless Olympic Peninsula. The Canadian-held Vancouver Island lies just north of the peninsula, across the Strait of Juan de Fuca.

The little communities of La Center, Ridgefield, and Ariel, lying along the Columbia just downstream from Portland, are typical of this southern region of Washington. In the middle of what was once a busy logging center, La Center was a major port for paddle wheelers. It is now home to a burgeoning wine industry,

The oldest church in Washington, Claquato Church **left** near Chehalis, wasn't just for worship. It was also a schoolhouse and a rest-stop for early pioneers.

The **wild turkey**, much more streamlined than the domesticated fowl bred for eating, lives chiefly in forests and broken woodland.

One of several examples of "carpenter's Gothic," the Henderson home in Tumwater **right** is in a specially designated historic district of the city.

with Salishan Vineyards offering both tours and a tasting room. Ridgefield, three miles east of La Center on the short Lake River (most rivers in Washington are short, unlike Oregon's) near its confluence with the Columbia, is near the site of an old Indian fishing village. The Lancaster House, built in 1850, is a surprisingly sophisticated example of Greek Revival architecture constructed under primitive conditions. Nestled between two wildlife refuges, the town offers both access to wildlife viewing and the river which boasts sturgeon, steelhead, bass, and catfish. The wildlife refuges, comprising three thousand acres between them, support migrating birds and offer good opportunities for bird-watching and photography via a vast network of trails and an observation blind.

Kelso (together with Longview) is the largest city-complex in this lower Columbia area. Built mostly on sawmill profits, it was the legendary smelt runs of the Cowlitz River that really put Kelso on the map. Needless to say, smelt along with an abundance of sturgeon and steelhead attract sportfishermen to this town. The old "Nat Smith" house, built in 1885 by a sawmill owner, is an excellent restored representation of middle-class aspirations. Kelso has a good approach to Mount St. Helens and the Gifford Pinchot National Forest. Visitors can learn how to move mountains as well as obtain updated road information and evacuation routes at the Kelso Volcano Interpretative Center.

On short detour to the west from Kelso along SR 4, paralleling the Columbia, are the small communities of Grays River, Skamokawa, and Cathlamet. Grays River features Washington's only covered bridge, the oldest remaining such bridge in the Pacific Northwest. First erected in 1905 as an uncovered span, the locals were soon forced to bow to the elements and a few years later it was covered. It still serves as a public road, covered. A few miles east of Grays River is Skamokawa, evocative of the nineteenth-century river towns once common along this stretch of the river. Formerly known as "little Venice" because it was built on stilts over the water, the town is now a historic district with its many old homes fronting onto Skamokawa Creek. Back toward Kelso along SR 4 is the riverside village of Cathlamet. You can take a trip on the last remaining ferry on the lower Columbia from nearby Puget Island. Referred to as "little Norway" because of its original settlers, Cathlamet is also the gateway to the 4,800-acre Columbia White-Tailed Deer National Wildlife Refuge. These deer, believed to be extinct in the 1930s, can best be viewed either from the refuge or from several nearby country roads. Early morning and dusk are good times to find the deer quietly grazing in the meadows of the refuge.

The rolling hills surrounding Centralia and Chehalis are home to both logging and dairying operations set in the rich Chehalis Valley. Centralia was founded in 1875 by George Washington, one of a handful of black pioneers, after being freed and adopted as a son by his Missouri master. Just west of Chehalis is the Claquato Church, built in 1858, with a tree planted outside the day Lincoln was assassinated. It is Washington's oldest church and has a splendid Crown of Thorns steeple, reminiscent of the mid-nineteenth-century New England churches on which it was patterned.

Skirting the Black Hills, I-5 heads north from the Chehalis Valley to the city of Tumwater, often referred to as the end of the Oregon Trail (but so are several other locations in the Pacific Northwest). It is probably better known today for its artesian waters. The brewing qualities of the water in the Deschutes River valley have been used advantageously for making Olympia Beer since 1895. Now designated a historic district, Tumwater was founded in 1845 and was the first permanent white settlement north of Fort Vancouver on the Columbia. The town has several examples of "Carpenter's Gothic" as well as the ancestral home of the state of Washington's favorite son, the late Bing Crosby.

Just north of Tumwater is the state capital, Olympia. Situated at the southern end of Puget Sound, the classically designed capitol buildings have been described by no less an authority than the editors of *American Architect* magazine as "reminiscent of the Acropolis at Athens." The grounds of the capitol command an impressive view of southern Puget Sound and the Olympic Mountains to the west.

Although the beds are privately owned, oyster cognoscenti should make a beeline for the bays north of Olympia on Puget Sound— Mud, Oyster, and Big and Little Skookum, where the tiny, delectable Olympia oysters are

harvested. If you are brave (or inebriated) try some raw on the half-shell in one of Olympia's many fine seafood restaurants. Just east of Olympia is Nisqually National Wildlife Refuge, preserving the ecology of the area's salt- and freshwater marshes, tidal flats, and swamps. Over seven miles of trails make this refuge a delight for bird-watchers, explorers, and photographers (cars and pets are understandably forbidden).

The Olympic Peninsula

Olympia is also the gateway to the Olympic Highway (101), which traverses Washington's wild Olympic Peninsula. Located in the northwest corner of the state, this peninsula is a combination of surf-pounded sandy beaches on its western edge and picturesque marine communities lining Puget Sound along its eastern and northern borders. In the middle are the richly carpeted rain forests, subalpine

meadows, and jagged mountain peaks draped in glaciers that make up the Olympic National Park.

While white settlers pushed bravely on into most of the rest of the Pacific Northwest, the Olympic Peninsula was another story entirely. No whites ventured very far up its rivers or into its impenetrable forests until recent years. As far as the outside world was considered, the Quinault Indians and the Hoh Indians were completely inaccessible which no doubt suited them. The only tenuous toeholds were eventually established along the peninsula's northern and eastern fringes, facing the Strait of Juan de Fuca and Puget Sound, respectively. And the peninsula remains nearly as inviolate to this day.

As a United Nations–designated World Heritage Area, the park is kept free of development, allowing life in the various ecosystems to continue as it has for millions of years. The result is that the park fairly teems with wildlife. Hikers may encounter some of the more famous residents of the area: Roosevelt elk (the park boasts the largest wild herd in its original setting in the world), and perhaps a bear, black-tailed deer, or the imperious bald eagle. One of three national parks within Washington's borders, Olympic National Park is the only park in the United States to encompass primitive coastline, rain forests and glaciered mountain slopes—including the lowest glaciers at this latitude in the world. Although virtually closed to vehicular traffic, two spur roads off Highway 101, west of Port Angeles, bring views of the magnificent Olympic range. "Heart o' the Hills" Highway climbs to 5,700 feet at Hurricane Ridge, and another road leads to Lake Quinault and Sol Duc Hot Springs. The Upper Hoh Road on the west side of the park is completely paved and leads through a lush rain forest where moss-draped Douglas fir and Sitka spruce attain towering heights of 300 feet or more. A trail of the same name provides access to the 5,000-foot glacier meadows and the Blue Glacier—a two-mile-wide ice slab—and only one of seven flanking Mount Olympus.

Close to 150 inches of rain annually drench this forest and you can understand why it is called the "Land of Green Twilight." Diffused light shrouded by the dense undergrowth and forest creates the soft green illumination of the most primeval rain forest.

Modeled along the classic lines of Athens' Acropolis, the Washington state capitol building **above** also looks uncannily like the federal capitol complex in Washington, D.C.

A hiking trail follows the Hoh River **left** for 18 miles, making this one of the most accessible areas in the Olympic National Park.

The **ferriginous hawk**, easily identifiable by its bright white underparts and reddish legs, is usually spotted perched on a tree, fencepost or rocky outcrop.

THE EASTERN REGIONS

The **Lawson cypress** was discovered on the Oregon/California boundary in 1854 by a Scotsman named Peter Lawson. It has more than 250 varieties and has become the most popular ornamental conifer.

Oregon's answer to Yellowstone, "Old Perpetual" in Lakeview **right** is the state's only constantly erupting geyser.

Opposite The Colville River doglegs through the forested country of Washington's Inland Empire.

The eastern section of the Pacific Northwest is sparsely populated (compared to other portions of this region), with few roads, not many sizable towns, and even fewer tourists. Indeed, although Washington's "Inland Empire" and its Palouse country are slightly better known, many staunch Oregonians would be hard-pressed to tell you much about the eastern section of their state.

Yet it is a region of unparalleled natural beauty from the vast, open rangeland of southeastern Oregon to the forested wilderness of northeastern Washington. You might have to slow down and drive more country roads—or even try a horseback trip—but visitors are well rewarded for their perseverance.

Southeastern Oregon

Southeastern Oregon is so huge and the population so sparse that it is hard to believe Americans fought first the Indians and then one another over this land. Yet the area's history records several Indian battles and, later, violent conflicts between ranchers and homesteaders during the massive land-grab of the mid- to late-nineteenth-century. The state's three largest counties are included in this wide, open space, covering some 28,450 square miles of high-desert plateau with a total population of 42,850 souls.

The state's advertising tag line, "Discover Surprising Oregon," takes on new meaning here. In this region you can explore the alkaline remains of the ancient seabed that once covered the entire western half of the continent. Flat-topped buttes, jutting spires, and rugged rimrock canyons evoke the Old West. The unusual geology includes Oregon's only continuously spouting geyser, "Old Perpetual," in Lakeview. This is cowboy country and is characterized by western hospitality, rodeos, and the largest ranching operations to be found anywhere in the United States.

Serious explorers can find thunder eggs as well as moss and white plume agates, jasper, petrified wood, sun stones, and obsidian. Fishing and boating opportunities abound far from the crowds, and unpublicized white-water trips are guided between the multicolored canyon walls of the desert river, the Owyhee. In the fall wild game, including chukar, quail, mule deer, and pheasant, attract hunters.

Starting in the southeastern portion of Oregon, Jordan Valley is the center of a region originally settled by Basque immigrants from the French and Spanish Pyrenees. Initially a way station on the frontier "freight line," the town is surrounded by remnants of relatively recent volcanic eruptions with large deposits of obsidian and weird geological formations as well as vast tracts of cattle and sheep ranches.

Paralleling the Oregon-Idaho border, and lying almost due north of Jordan Valley, is the town of Nyssa—self-proclaimed as the Thunder egg Capital of Oregon. More importantly, Nyssa is the gateway to the Owyhee canyon lands. Lake Owyhee fills thirty-five miles of the canyon and has been described by happy anglers as "the most overstocked and underfished lake in America."

West of Nyssa, at the junction of US 395 and US 20, is Burns, the business center for Oregon's "Big Country" with its vast ranches, Steen Mountain range, and Malheur Lake nearby. The lake is a major nesting and feeding stop on the Pacific Flyway, and nearly 250 species have been counted in this 183,000-acre refuge.

Northeastern Oregon was the scene of the last great Indian resistance in Oregon. The Nez Percés, led by their brilliant strategist and peacetime spokesman, Chief Joseph, were forcibly evicted from their lands in 1877. Declaring that "All men were made by the same Great Spirit. They are all brothers. The earth is the mother of all people, and all people should have equal rights to it," Chief Joseph led his people on a pathetic thousand-mile odyssey to avoid confinement to the federal reservation. Starvation and continual army harassment finally forced Joseph to surrender, and he finished his days on the Colville reservation of northern Washington. His one dying wish—to be buried in his homeland—has never been granted.

Gold, not fertile land, led to this section's settlement. And until gold was discovered in the Blue and Wallowa mountains in 1861, immigrants were just passing through. You can follow the Oregon Trail (now I-84) through this vast mountainous, canyon-carved region. Two mountain ranges, acres of wheat fields, and huge range land, all fed by deep rivers, define the geography. You can ski in the Anthony Lakes area, search for vanished gold-mining boomtowns, ride the white water or retreat to some sedate fishing on an alpine lake.

The Wallowas Area

The Wallowas are referred to by the locals as the "Switzerland of America"; you will understand why the Nez Percés stood and fought rather than voluntarily give up their beautiful country. Take a boat trip through 6,000-foot-deep Hell's Canyon for a close-up view of the

"Bulldogging" **above** is one of the timed events in rodeo; it involves a sane man trying to drag 700 pounds of steer to the ground. Horse and rider burst out of the gate in hot pursuit of a racing steer; the cowboy leaps from his saddle onto the animal, digs his heels in, stops the steer and deposits his quarry in the dirt—all in less than five seconds.

Looking out from Mount Howard across the Wallowa range, this view **left** helps the visitor understand why the Nez Percé Indians were reluctant to be moved.

This **goldminers' candle-holder** of the 1860s is made of wrought iron. It was called a "sticking tommy" by the miners, who hammered it directly into the walls of the mineshaft.

105

The **moose**, largest of the deer family, is found in coniferous forests, but is especially fond of swampy land, where it feeds on the roots and stems of aquatic plants like the water-lily.

canyon's unique ecology and geology and some ancient Indian petroglyphs. Guided fishing excursions from the town appropriately named Halfway will take you to pools inhabited by the largest freshwater fish—white sturgeon.

West of Hell's Canyon on I-84, the town of Baker grew into a thriving trade center when stories of a stream pebbled by gold nuggets reached the outside world in 1861. Today it still thrives as base to ranchers and lumbermen. Its distinctive architecture of towers and spires in a snow-capped mountain setting is reminiscent of a European village. In late July, Baker holds its annual Miners' Jubilee, where contests include gold-panning, races, and a parade.

Southwest of Baker at the junction of US 26 and US 395 the town of John Day still witnesses cattle drives down its main street. Many ghost towns and abandoned mine shafts are in the hills surrounding John Day, notably Canyon City and Prairie City.

For the biggest, most genuine rodeo in the Pacific Northwest do NOT miss Pendleton during the annual Round-Up week in September. Begun in 1910, this rodeo brings in competitors from across the country, and spectators can watch the meanest four-footed creatures compete against the toughest two-footed cowboys. An associated event is presented by the Northwest Indian tribes and features a huge tepee encampment and ceremonial dancing.

Walla Walla, in the southeastern corner of Washington, is an area laden with history. An important resting place on the Oregon Trail before the final push through the Columbia Gorge and later a destination in itself, the city today is the commercial center for the surrounding agricultural area. Nestled between the Blue Mountains to the south and east and the Columbia Basin on the west, the Walla Walla valley is an oasis of rich, green farmland. Despite Al Jolson's crack that Walla Walla was "the city they liked so well they named it twice," in fact the Indian word means "many waters."

In 1836 the American Board of Commissioners for Foreign Missions despatched Dr. Marcus Whitman and his wife Narcissa to the Waiilatpu country—"the people of the place of the rye grass"—to bring God and civilization to the Cayuse Indians. The Indians, initially interested in the white man's god, grew sullen at the Whitmans' insistence that in order to glorify God they would have to settle and farm. As Narcissa noted in her journal, "One said it was good when they knew nothing but to hunt, eat, drink and sleep; now it was bad." In 1847 the Cayuse rose up and massacred most of the white adults at the mission. When news of the massacre reached an alarmed Congress, federal troops were despatched to punish the Cayuse and pack them off to a reservation, but not before one of their chiefs, Tomahas, and two warriors had surrendered and been hanged for the "crime." In a touching bit of irony, when asked why they had given themselves up, Tomahas responded that Dr. Whitman had taught him that chiefs such as Christ willingly died to protect their people—so he, Tomahas, was willing to protect his tribe from the barbarity of the United States Army.

White settlers began arriving on the heels of the federal troops once the area had been cleared of rebellious Indians. The landscape today is one of vast rolling wheat fields stretching to the horizon, neat red and white barns, stands of cottonwoods tracing the course of streams. It is Washington's "Inland Empire," and, like Oregon's eastern edge, it is relatively unknown.

Modern Walla Walla is a city of parks, including historic Fort Walla Walla, one of the earliest fortifications in the region offering sanctuary to pioneers. Just west of the city is the Whitman National Historic Site, but all that remains of the once thriving mission is a marker detailing the tragedy of 1847.

East of Walla Walla is Washington's section of the Umatilla National Forest, in the Blue Mountains. Fishing in streams inhabited by rainbow trout, salmon, and steelhead and hunting for elk and mule deer are possible, and camping and hiking facilities are plentiful. Bluewood is an excellent ski area in the Blue Mountains nearby.

West of Walla Walla, along what was once the Lewis and Clark Trail, is Sacajawea State Park, situated at the confluence of the Snake and Columbia rivers. Named in honor of Lewis and Clark's celebrated Indian guide, the park has an excellent interpretative center featuring the expedition and local Indian history. Visitors arriving in this Tri-Cities (Kennewick-Pasco-Richland) area in late July should take

Sheep Rock provides a fine
backdrop to the John Day River in Oregon's
John Day Fossil Beds National
Monument. Fossil evidence dated at 30
million years old has put this
region on the anthropologist's map.

The **peregrine falcon**, one of the world's fastest-flying birds, preys on other birds. It uses its talons to seize its victims and is one of the few birds to strike in mid-air.

in the annual Water Follies, ten days of activities climaxing with hydroplane races on the Columbia River. Palouse Falls at Washtucna (west of Pullman) is a spectacular two-hundred-foot-high waterfall cascading down onto a semi-arid plateau of rocks and outcroppings. During the Ice Age the Palouse River emptied into the Snake River near the present-day city of Pasco. Glacial floods, however, filled the valley and altered its course, causing it to cross the divide and cut a deep spillway before entering the Snake River farther upstream. A series of waterfalls formed, but only Palouse Falls remains today.

North of Washtucna is the Russian-German town of Ritzville, famous for the home of Dr. Frank Burroughs. If the high cost of today's medical care staggers, you'll be impressed by what two dollars could buy of Dr. Burroughs's services. This pioneer physician's office contains records of calls made on patients, fees charged, and a record of the babies delivered (a sizable number).

The Grand Coulee Dam Region

Northwest of Ritzville is Washington's coulee country—huge canyons, dammed by the granddaddy of them all, Grand Coulee Dam; a recreational paradise, a geologist's dream, an absolute requirement for the agriculture in the Columbia Basin. As the Ice Age drew to a close the melt formed a huge river—the largest ever known—that began carving its channels and coulees through the ancient lava beds, including one spectacular plunge 400 feet across a three-mile-wide chasm now known as Dry Falls. Two of the largest coulees, Moses Coulee and Grand Coulee, were left high and dry as the waters receded, and it is the latter, Grand Coulee, which is today inundated by the great dam. Golf courses, boating, fishing lakes, and excellent swimming are available all along the coulee region from Moses Lake in the south through Sun Lakes and on to the vast Roosevelt Lake jutting north as far as Kettle Falls. The evidence of glaciation in this area makes it ideal territory for budding geologists.

Archaeologists can explore for Indian artifacts—human habitation of this region is dated back 9,000 years.

The brainchild of an enterprising central Washington editor, Grand Coulee Dam is a technological as well as an ecological symbol. An eight-year WPA project begun in 1933, the dam was designed to divert the Columbia back into its original Ice Age channels to supply energy, flood control, and that necessity of the Inland Empire—irrigation. Immortalized in Woody Guthrie's "Roll on, Columbia," the dam has literally brought new life to a million acres of arid land. The visitor's center on the west bank gives a concise explanation of this mammoth concrete structure, and tours of the powerhouse, pump stations, and even the top of the dam itself start from here. The giant spillway is illuminated at night in a sound and light show during the summer.

Contrasted to the rugged region south of the dam, the long arm of Roosevelt Lake (the Columbia impounded behind the dam) is an area of beaches and water recreation opportunities. Boaters can cruise the lake all the way to British Columbia, camping at night along the shore.

Spokane and Environs

East of Grand Coulee Dam is the commercial heart of the Inland Empire, Spokane. Spokane House, established by the North West Company of fur trappers in 1810, became the first white settlement in the Pacific Northwest and the foundation of modern Spokane.

Spokane is also a gateway to recreation possibilities. The water recreation areas of the Idaho Panhandle are less than 30 miles east. Roosevelt Lake is just to the west. Skiers in this part of the state head for Mount Spokane, about 20 miles northeast in the Colville and Kaniksu national forests. The numerous lakes and streams of the forest near the Canadian border draw anglers during early summer in pursuit of rainbow and cutthroat trout. Also of interest here is the limestone cavern at Crawford State Park.

Previous page Site of Expo '74, Spokane's Riverfront Park sparkles in its nighttime dress of illuminations.

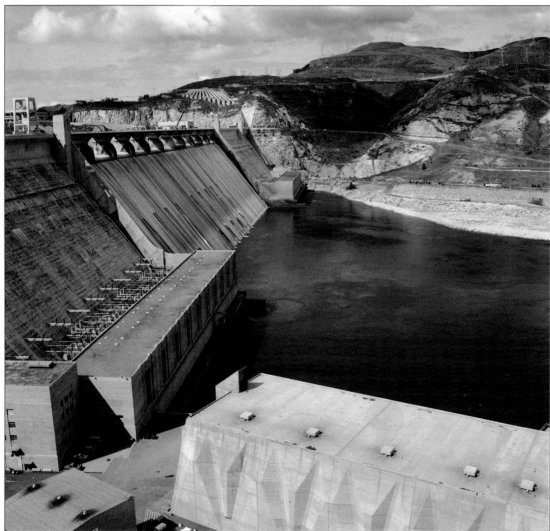

The sun-washed tranquility of Roosevelt Lake, Washington, is a boater's paradise **above**. This ribbon of lake—actually the Columbia penned behind Grand Coulee Dam—stretches as far north as Canada.

Vital to the economy of central Washington, the Grand Coulee Dam **left** ranks as one of the wonders of the world and is immortalized in Woodie Guthrie's "Roll on Columbia" as "the mightiest thing ever built by a man."

Northwest of Spokane is the Colville Indian Reservation, largest in the state and home today of the Nez Percés. Intertribal war dances every January and an Indian Days celebration in September are held in the town of Wellpinit on the reservation. Nespelem is the site of the grave of Chief Joseph, last great leader of the Nez Percés.

On the western edge of the reservation, Omak hosts one of the largest Indian celebrations in the state, along with the legendary Omak Stampede and Suicide Race every August.

Okanogan National Forest recreation facilities border the reservation on its northern edge. The small village of Republic is home to Knob Hill Mine, richest and largest gold-producing mine in the Pacific Northwest. Prospecting for gold and silver is still going on today, and these hills are dotted with the remains of nineteenth-century mining towns.

To the east of Okanogan Forest on the eastern banks of Roosevelt Lake is the Kettle Falls Archaeological District, including major sites related to historic and prehistoric occupations here. These sites represent approximately 9,000 years of trading contact among several Indian tribes. This is also the site of the Hudson's Bay Company post at Fort Colville and a Jesuit mission of Saint Paul's. Bear in mind, too, that it was in this vicinity that the tracks of the crippled Bigfoot were found, giving the first scientific substantiation to the existence of the huge creature.

111

MOUNT ST. HELENS

*F*or the utterly jaded or complacent, Mount St. Helens presents a must-see item on any visit to the Pacific Northwest. As volcanic eruptions go, Mount St. Helens's was not massive, yet its movement and long-term effects must rate right up there with cataclysmic, perception-altering experiences.

Before Mount St. Helens gave us the first volcanic event in the contiguous 48 states in 63 years it was the quintessential mountain. Evocative of comparisons to Japan's Mount Fuji, its towering forested slopes climaxed in a near-perfect cone topped by a clean mantle of year-round snow. Located in the popular Gifford Pinchot National Forest, its slopes were home to Roosevelt elk, black bears, cougars, black-tailed deer, and mountain goats. The beautiful Spirit Lake, so named by the Indians because a strange moaning arose from its depths, located at the mountain's base, was stocked with trout annually. Massive 150-foot high Douglas firs and other conifers populated its forest—indeed, Weyerhaeuser Lumber Company owns logging rights to much of the area subsequently devasted in the eruption. It is this rugged, isolated country that the legendary Bigfoot purportedly roams and into which D. B. Cooper parachuted out of a hijacked airplane in 1971, with $200,000 in marked bills, never to be heard from since (although several thousand of his currency has been recovered).

Part of the Pacific "Ring of Fire," a series of active and dormant volcanoes surrounding the Pacific Ocean, and one of several in the Cascade Range, Mount St. Helens is more aptly described by the Cowlitz Indian name of "Louwala-Clough" or "Fire Mountain." According to Indian legend, two competing suitors, "Wyest" and "Klickitat," got into a spat over the charms of a beautiful maiden, "Loowit." As the impetuous warriors hurled fiery rocks at each other, burning villages and forests, "Sahala," the Great Spirit, became so angered that he turned the three into rock. Because Loowit was beautiful, her mountain (Saint Helens) was a beautiful, symmetrical cone of dazzling white. Wyest (Mount Hood) lifts his head in pride, but Klickitat (Mount Adams) weeps to see his beautiful maiden wrapped forever in snow, so he bends his head as he gazes on Saint Helens.

A baby in geological time, Saint Helens in about a million years old. Since 400 B.C. the mountain has alternated long dormant periods with cycles of eruptions. When it began to rumble early in 1980, core drilling revealed the mountain was a "strato" volcano made up of alternating layers of unstable ash and lava concealing a still older volcano between 2,500 and 40,000 years old. Prehistoric man crossing the Bering Strait landmass exposed during the last Ice Age was probably terrorized by this earlier incarnation of Mount St. Helens. With repeated eruptions of lava, cooling and building in layers, the upper portion of the near-perfect cone actually developed just 400 years ago.

Prior to its 1980 eruption, Mount St. Helens had been the most *active* of the Cascades' volcanoes, most recently venting for 26 years beginning in 1831. Mount Lassen, another Cascades peak, in northern California, had been the most recent active volcano in the contiguous 48 states—it vented for three years starting in 1915.

The Eruption

In March 1980 Mount St. Helens began to wake up, venting small bursts of steam and ash in minor eruptions. By March 28 a second crater opened up beside the first and the two merged into a bowl 1,700 feet across and 850 feet deep. By now United States Geological Survey teams were in the area. All the mountain's previously pristine white crown was now dirty, and its north side began to swell at a rate of five feet a day. All systems were on alert, and in a marvelous example of bureaucratic-speak the geologists deemed the eruption level of the mountain "low energy mode."

In addition to its flora and fauna, Mount St. Helens was also home to the now legendary Harry R. Truman, 84 cantankerous years of age in 1980. Living for 50 years in a guest lodge he had built beside Spirit Lake in the shadow of the mountain, Harry resolutely refused to be evacuated. Raising the adjectival use of

Fishermen on Frog Lake **right** enjoy the majesty of Mount Hood, Oregon's premier peak.

Previous page After the 1980 eruption: trees six feet and more in diameter lie flattened over thousands of acres of moonscape surrounding Mount Saint Helens.

expletives to an art form, Harry peppered the news reports with his mostly unprintable direct quotes that would embarrass any marine and make his namesake, Harry S. Truman, blush. Various members of the media, covering the by-then rumbling mountain, regularly trekked to Harry's lodge for his version of the Pioneer Spirit and the American way. The entire school body of Clear Lake Elementary School adopted him, writing letters begging him to flee to safety. But Harry would not be moved, vowing "Hell, no, I ain't leavin' ... I'm goin' to set right here and watch the show."

Meanwhile, in the surrounding towns the great American entrepreneurial spirit was coming to the forefront. T-shirts and bumper stickers were marketed with such punishing puns on "ash" as "Get Your Ash Together," "Excuse My Ash," and "St. Helens—Keep Your Ash Off My Lawn." Local wags dubbed the mountain "Old Shake and Bake."

But on Sunday morning, May 18, 1980, all the joking stopped. At 8:30 A.M. an earthquake registering 5.0 jolted the mountain. Two minutes later the entire north face, half a mile wide and a mile from top to bottom, blew out in an unexpected horizontal direction. The blast and shock waves destroyed a fan-shaped area eight miles long and 15 miles wide along the north side of the peak, causing a massive landslide toward the North Toutle River. Boiling volcanic gases and steam shot out through the gashed side of the mountain, trashing forests 18 miles away. Shots of searing hot ash and rocks gushed 400 million tons of debris skyward 60,000 feet into the air, surrounded by lightning bolts timed at six per minute. The roar of gases could be heard 200 miles away. Winds took the plume east to Yakima, 85 miles away, creating an eery midnight blackness at 9:30 A.M. that would last the entire day. Two-

hundred-miles-per-hour winds hurtled debris and scalding mud down the mountain, flattening some 3.2 billion board feet of once-proud Douglas firs. Melting ice caused an estimated 46 billion gallons of water to plummet down the mountainside, creating mudflows and floods. Boulders, bulldozers, locomotives, and giant logging trucks were carelessly hurtled around like so many children's toys. Avalanches overwhelmed rivers, towns, and a portion of Interstate Highway 5. By midday ashfall had brought most of eastern Washington, northern Idaho, and western Montana staggering blindly to a halt. With winds blowing to the east the giant ash cloud reached the Atlantic Ocean three days later. The Columbia River, second most powerful in the country, was so heavily blocked by silt that it was closed to deep-draft vessles. At one point a 40-foot channel was reduced to fourteen feet. Volcanic silt was so heavy that ordinary sonar equipment could not take soundings and the Army Corps of Engineers had to call in helicopters equipped with weighted lines to determine depths.

The Aftermath

When the smoke cleared, search parties were quickly organized and miraculously rescued 198 people. It was estimated that two million birds, fish, and animals had died, twenty-six lakes were destroyed, and 150 miles of streams were gone. Weyerhaeuser found themselves in possession of 230 square miles of clear-cut timber, a great deal of it salvage-

able. Fifty-seven people were dead or missing. Harry R. Truman had been buried along with his beloved lodge, fifteen cats, and a large stock of Jack Daniels.

The mountain itself had blasted away over 1,300 feet of its own crest, reducing its elevation to 8,364 feet. Because of the amount of energy the eruption generated, comparisons are inevitable to other instances of exploded energy. Mount St. Helens equaled 500 Hiroshimas, or 5,000 times the amount of TNT dropped on Dresden, Germany, in 1945. Or to go farther back in history, the U.S. Geological Survey reported that the mountain spewed forth a total of 143,500 cubic feet of volcanic materials—almost equal to that which covered Pompeii after the eruption of Vesuvius in A.D. 79.

Besides remodeling and shaping its immediate environment the erupting volcano has had more far-reaching effects. Some scientists believe that fine volcanic ash high in the atmosphere regulates solar heat and energy affecting the long-term climatic pattern. The ubiquitous glass-sharded ash, besides damaging crops and machinery when farmers attempted to plow it under, has also made it tough going for crop-destroying insects such as grasshoppers. In fact, soil is enhanced by volcanic ash—fruit growers of the Wenatchee Valley have for years touted their product as

"grown deep in volcanic soil."

Biologists, botanists, and entomologists *as well as* geologists converged on the site once the dust cleared. The nutrient-rich waters of re-formed Spirit Lake and the ash-covered earth offer a living laboratory for researchers. Scientists can go back in time to study various life-forms' responses from "day one". The Army Corps of Engineers has erected new dams and levees and dredged new channels. U.S. Forest Service personnel have co-ordinated efficient alert and evacuation procedures that are models for other potential disaster areas. And the U.S. Geological Survey team believes it can now accurately predict volcanic eruptions to within a workable margin.

All of which preparation is necessary. Because as you read this the cooling and layering of lava within the mountain is again building at the rate of 20 feet per day, and the geologists tell us Mount St. Helens is once again in the dome-building phase. Based on the mountain's past performance we can expect this latest period of eruptions to continue until at least the year 2010.

Early colonizers in the denuded environment around Mount Saint Helens, vivid spring flowers **above left** bloom today as Mother Earth re-establishes her supremacy after the destructive eruption.

A tall, symmetrical snow-clad peak **below left** domating the skyline . . . mountain of geologic youth . . . these are memories of Mount Saint Helens, shown here at sunrise.

THE
CENTRAL REGION

*I*f you're tired of the "ever wet" western sections of the Pacific Northwest, this sun-drenched country in the central part of the region—ranging from the juniper and sagebrush of southern Oregon to Washington's irrigated Yakima and Wenatchee valleys—will warm your bones. With the Cascades forming a formidable barrier, residents in central Oregon and Washington regard Indian summer almost as a fifth season.

Central Oregon

The terrain of central Oregon is similar to that of western Oregon, only drier. Geographically, central Oregon is blessed with more than 220 lakes and 235 miles of rivers and streams. The region's main waterway is the Deschutes River (so named by French-Canadian trappers who were impressed by its many waterfalls), which begins in the Cascades southwest of Bend and parallels the east slopes of the range to the Columbia. White-water adventurers as well as anglers find plenty of activity on the Deschutes. Hikers, campers, skiers, and boaters will enjoy the vast recreational reaches of the Deschutes National Forest. In fact, downhill skiers will find world-class facilities open into late summer on the east side of the Cascades. Central Oregon is also a region beloved of rock hounds—thunder eggs, agates, and other semiprecious stones can be found around the town of Prineville.

It was a Hudson's Bay Company explorer, Peter Skene Ogden later to place his name forever in the history of the region by rescuing the kidnapped survivors of the Whitman Mission massacre), who first traveled through this area in the mid-1820s. In fact, the entire region was so crisscrossed with Indian trails that early white explorers had an easy time following well-established Indian trading routes. One of the main trails leading from the Columbia River south followed the Deschutes River; in 1843 a major military exploration led by Captain John C. Frémont and guided by Kit Carson headed south from Fort Dalles in search of the "Multnomah River." It was hoped that this river, which turned out to be mythical, would flow through the Cascades into the Willamette valley. Today U.S. 97, as it heads south from The Dalles, follows the approximate route of Frémont's expedition, taking a short side trip into Dufur and then following a county road to Wapinitia and Simnasho to what is now the Warm Springs Indian Reservation.

The protection of Indians' rights was sometimes a concern of the U.S. Army, and in the early part of the nineteenth-century white settlement east of the Cascades was forbidden. But in 1858 a gold boom in eastern Oregon and Idaho demanded a change in policy, and central Oregon was soon crisscrossed with supply-train routes. Today you can follow some of these old supply routes on modern highways, notably US 20 and SR 126.

Regardless of which highway you take you will come to the town of Sisters, named long before women's liberation was even a gleam in the eye of Gloria Steinem (for those concerned about such things there is also a town in Oregon called Brothers). Founded at the turn of the century, the town has assumed an antique appearance evocative of the Old West, complete with genuine hitching posts. Sisters State Park, on the community's fringe, occupies the meeting point of major Indian trails from the south, north, and west. Sisters' rodeo, held in mid-June, is regarded as one of the state's best small exhibitions. And the town is within 25 miles of the Black Butte resort area, the Metolius River (which features a "fly-fishing only" zone in its upper ten-mile stretch), and the Hoodoo Ski Bowl at the summit of Santiam Pass.

Travel on the wagon roads soon led to the development of the towns east of Sisters: Prineville, Redmond, and Bend. Bend became an important crossroads because of its location on the east side of the Cascade passes and its strategic placement on the Oregon Central Military Road (now known as US 97). It is today this area's largest city. Oregon's largest ski facility at Mount Bachelor is only 22 miles west, and superb trout-fishing is less than an hour away. East of Bend is an extinct volcano known as Pilot Butte, and one who climbs to its summit is rewarded with a sweeping view of nine snow-capped Cascade peaks.

The Oregon High Desert Museum on US 97,

Opposite This famous portion of the Columbia River Gorge, which interrupts the Cascades between Portland and The Dalles, is a scenic wonder of tremendous conservational, historical and recreational importance.

Hikers are attracted by the lofty views of the Cascades from the 6,415-foot summit of Black Butte **center** on the eastern fringe of the Deschutes National Forest.

a few miles south of Bend, is devoted primarily to natural rather than human history. The museum does have "living history" exhibits of Indian culture as well as displays on the Oregon's high desert's relationship with the region's homesteaders and pioneer loggers.

Continuing a short way south from the museum is the Lava Lands Visitor Center at the base of five-hundred-foot Lava Butte. The Center provides a graphic aid to your imagination: automated tremors and dramatic visual displays help visitors understand this area's volcanic history. Ancient Mount Newberry, the source of the ancient lava flows, has within its giant crater one of the world's largest obsidian flows and two scenic lakes—Paulina and East.

Northeast of Bend on US 26 is the area's oldest town, Prineville, founded in 1868 on the banks of the Crooked River. From its earliest days Prineville earned a reputation for being one of the wildest of Oregon's frontier towns, and its local museum chronicles the state's bloodiest range war, a conflict between sheep and cattle ranchers. The Crooked River, passing near town, is a prime rock-hounding area. The Prineville Reservoir, 25 miles south of town on the Crooked River, is recognized as one of Oregon's premier bass waters; cutthroat trout and catfish can also be caught here. Gold was supposedly first discovered east of the Cascades along this river by a search party looking for a lost wagon train. To their credit the search party went on to rescue the starving wagon party, thereby losing the gold discovery. However, continued searches eventually led to gold strikes in the Blue Mountains in eastern Oregon in the 1860s.

North of Prineville, along US 26, is the Warm Springs Indian Reservation. One of Frémont's discoveries was the hot springs incorporated into today's Kah-Nee-Ta resort, a reservation formed in 1855 through treaties with the Wasco and Walla Walla tribes. Today the resort caters to visitors who want a vacation with an Indian theme: seasonal activities include Indian dances and storytelling. The tiny town of Tygh Valley, north of Warm Springs, features wild horses from the reservation in its annual mid-May Pacific Northwest Championship All-Indian Rodeo. In spring the reservation's portion of the Deschutes River is part of a chinook salmon run, and in summer the fighting steelhead can be caught here.

The Columbia River

Fed by the melting of glaciers high in the Canadian Rockies, the Columbia River quickly becomes a mighty thoroughfare in its dash to the Pacific, second only to the Mississippi on the North American continent. But it was the terrifying narrow Columbia River Gorge that first put the river on the maps of early explorers. The Lewis and Clark Expedition of

Thrills and spills are the order of the day for white-water rafters on the Deschutes River **left**, Oregon's major waterway.

Overleaf Many pioneers chose to settle in the vicinity of The Dalles not because of its scenic beauty but because of their fear of descending its rapids.

The river's course through the gorge with its scenic falls **right** was regarded as a beautiful but unforgiving obstacle to nineteenth-century fur traders and pioneers.

Now all that remains of an ancient forest, these stony logs **above** in Gingko Petrified Forest, central Washington, more closely resemble rocks today.

A few stalwart pines **left** find sustenance in the dry desolation of a lava flow at McKenzie Pass in Oregon's Cascades. If your imagination fails, the visitors' center features automated tremors and dramatic visual displays to help you understand the region's volcanic past.

1804–1805 was the first to chart the Columbia from its confluence with the Snake River to the Pacific Ocean. Excellent diarists, both men recorded their tribulations, from tangling with grizzly bears to the day their Shoshone Indian guide, Sacajawea, bore her first child mid-trail. Once on the Columbia the expedition wasted no time portaging around difficult rapids if they could ride the river faster. But when they reached the point where the river passes between steep cliffs just forty yards apart (near present-day The Dalles), their intent was sorely tested. Portaging was impossible along the precipitous cliffs on either side and the local Indians advised a wide detour around the dangerous rapids. But Lewis and Clark pressed on with their water route. "I was determined," wrote Clark, "to pass through this place notwithstanding the horrid appearance of this agitated gut swelling, boiling and whorling in every direction." And to the surprise of everyone, including the Indians who had gathered on the cliffs to witness the party's sure destruction, the explorers emerged downstream unscathed.

By 1821 Hudson's Bay Company and the North West Company had merged, and in 1824 a fort at Vancouver (across the river from Portland) was established. Under the stewardship of Dr. John McLoughlin, it was to become the largest Hudson's Bay Company post along the Pacific. McLoughlin, a Canadian, was responsible for strengthening the Hudson's Bay Company position in the entire region, at the time jointly administered by both the British and American governments. McLoughlin became increasingly disenchanted with his employers while becoming enamored of the American democratic system. He began to assist and actively encourage American immigration into the region along the Columbia. Even when the new arrivals brought their anti-black and anti-Indian prejudices (McLoughlin's wife was half Indian) and tried to seize company lands, McLoughlin remained steadfast in his newfound loyalties.

By 1843 the huge swell of immigrants began arriving in the Oregon country. With their six months' journey to the promised land of the Willamette valley nearly complete, the pioneers faced one more critical obstacle: the formidable Cascades. There was no practicable wagon route over, through, or around the mountains; the Columbia River offered the only way through to Fort Vancouver—from there it was just a day's journey to the Willamette valley.

"God never made a mountain but that He provided a place for man to go around it," declared Sam Barlow. And he did just that, building a toll road that allowed immigrants to go overland at The Dalles across the Cascades, thus avoiding the worst of the

Oregon boasts no less than four separate mountain ranges, all of which are mantled in snow at least part of the year. Skiing is a passion for many Oregonians and Mount Bachelor **right** offers the state's largest ski facilities, just 22 miles from Bend.

Columbia River Gorge (although the rest of the river journey was by no means without its dangers). But early travelers were obliged to stop at Fort Walla Walla just east of the gorge, there to build small boats or rafts, abandoning wagons and oxen—animals so well beloved by now that many hardy pioneers wept to say good-bye to their faithful animals.

In a later recollection Jesse Applegate, at the time seven years old, described the beginnings of his party's ordeal by river, expressing some of the foreboding felt by all: "I did see some ugly cliffs of rock, black and forbidding in appearance. ... neither did the grown-up people seem to be delighted with the scenery along the river." And indeed, the treacherous river at The Dalles was to claim many lives including those of two children of the Applegate party, just one day away from their final destination.

The barge traffic moving placidly through the Columbia Gorge today belies the risks earlier travelers faced in negotiating this stretch of the river before the construction of dams and navigational locks "tamed" it. Completed in 1896, these locks enabled river traffic to bypass the dangerous stretch of rapids with-out the necessity of portaging. The horrendous rapids described by Lewis and Clark are now submerged in the reservoir formed by the Bonneville Dam.

Just downstream from Portland is Sauvie Island at the confluence of the Willamette and Columbia rivers. Sauvie was the site of one of Lewis and Clark's camps as well as the location of Nathaniel Wyeth's short-lived fur-trading post, Fort William. Today the island has several beautiful old homes to tour, notably the Bybee-Howell House, a territorial homestead built in 1856.

The old Hudson's Bay Company Fort Vancouver is today the modern city of Vancouver, located at the head of deep-water navigation on the Columbia. The oldest city in Washington, Vancouver was principally a supply station in its early days—first to immigrants coming down the Columbia enroute to the Willamette and later to prospectors heading for the gold fields in eastern Oregon and Idaho.

Continuing east on the Washington side, the ports of Camas and Washougal offer excellent boating and angling opportunities: the Washougal River is well known for its steel-

head, whereas salmon and sturgeon are to be found here in the Columbia River.

Moving upstream from Washougal. The Bonneville Dam is the oldest on the Columbia and one of four massive U.S. Army Corps of Engineers projects along the Oregon-Washington border. Bradford Island, an ancient Indian burial ground, now houses an extensive visitor's center. Dam operations, navigational history, and fish migration are well illustrated. It is also possible to watch salmon "climbing" underwater fish ladders.

Just east of the dam is the legendary Bridge of the Gods, the connecting link between Washington and Oregon for the arduous Pacific Crest Trail. According to Indian lore a great natural stone bridge spanned the Columbia at this point. Irritated by the constantly warring mountains (Mount Hood and Mount Adams fighting over the charms of Mount St. Helens) the Great Spirit broke down the bridge, leaving it in pieces in the river below. The rocks of it can still be seen.

Just beyond the Bridge of the Gods lie the two small communities of Bingen and White Salmon, both giving scenic access to the

Visitors to the Bonneville Dam **left**, whose spillway is shown here, can also watch the barges and other river traffic negotiate the navigational locks above the dam.

Placid banks on either side of
the Columbia today belie the risks early
travelers faced before the
construction of dams and navigational locks
"tamed" this part of the river's
turbulence.

Washington side of the Gorge. Bingen was named by early German settlers because of the location's great resemblance to Bingen-on-the-Rhine, and today a Rhineland theme pervades the town, including a glockenspiel in a bell tower, billed as the only true glockenspiel west of the Mississippi.

On the Oregon side of the bridge is the city of Hood River, the gateway to the productive fruit-growing valley to the south where apple, pear, and cherry orchards predominate.

Blossom festival time in late April makes for especially scenic drives around this valley. Hood River hosts an old-fashioned Fourth of July celebration that features a sailboat regatta, and a Columbia River Cross-Channel Swim closes the summer as a Labor Day tradition.

Modern travelers can still follow the old Barlow road by driving on US 26 as it wraps around Mount Hood. Just below the old route, deep gashes still show on tree trunks where ropes were used to slow a wagon's descent. In the lower end of the gorge, the road still traverses some of the original "upper level" highway that made it accessible at the turn of the century.

The Dalles

Around a deep bend in the river is The Dalles. Known as "the end of the Oregon Trail" in the 1840s, the town was originally established as a fort. The name itself is a derivation of the French word meaning "flagstones," and earliest French-Canadian explorers were probably referring to the basalt-lined channels of the Columbia. These channels are today submerged under The Dalles Dam to the east of town. Today the city is a busy agricultural and shipping center for the eastern portion of Oregon. At The Dalles Dam visitors can tour the powerhouse and navigational locks and witness the migration of the salmon as they go up and over fish ladders. The short drive along Highway 84 between Mosier and Rowena gives a magnificent view of the gorge west of The Dalles with a 34-acre wildflower preserve along the way.

Lush ferns **above** proliferate alongside the Columbia River—witness to an ever-present abundance of moisture.

The magnificent Bridge of the Gods **below**, part of the Pacific Crest Trail, spans the Columbia between Washington and Oregon.

The Columbia cuts deep against a rugged cliff **overleaf** near The Dalles.

This **mountain hawk mask** is an example of the fine art produced by the Indians of the northwest. It was carved in wood by the Nisko tribe of British Columbia.

The Yakima and Wenatchee Valleys

North of the Columbia River Gorge are the two agricultural valleys of Washington: the Yakima and the Wenatchee. If the Willamette valley was the found Promised Land, then the Yakima-Wenatchee valley was the created Promised Land. Irrigation is the key that unlocked the vast agricultural wealth of these two valleys, and it was the Yakima Indians who first experimented with irrigation. In the heart of the Columbia Basin this near-desert country was as different as night and day from the evergreen region lying on the western side of the Cascades. But as rivers were dammed and irrigation channels dug (and the Indians removed), farmers began to settle in the region. By the late nineteenth century the valley was awash with the heady scent of fruit orchards where cattle had once died of starvation and thirst. Today central Washington is recognized as one of the most productive agricultural areas in the nation.

In the very southern end of this region an eccentric Seattle lawyer named Samuel Hill built a castle for his Rodin collection as well as an improbable concrete replica of Stonehenge. Both are to be found in Maryhill on the banks of the Columbia, 100 miles from the nearest major city. In addition to a fine collection of Rodin sculptures, there are art glass by Galle, icons, Indian artifacts, and a large assemblage of antique chess sets, all housed in a stately manor house complete with peacocks strutting regally around in the formal gardens. Maryhill, so reminiscent of an English country house, is all the more surprising as an introduction to an area famous for its cowboys and Indians.

Just a few miles north from Maryhill is in fact the Yakima Indian Reservation, the second largest in the state. Toppenish, on US 97, is the administrative center of the Yakima Nation as well as the headquarters for its cultural center and museum. Two miles south is the Toppenish National Wildlife Refuge, where more than 148 species of birds have been sighted. On the eastern side of the reservation are several of the state's newest wineries,

located in Grandview, Sunnyside, and Zillah. West of Toppenish is Fort Simcoe at White Swan. One of the two U.S. Army posts established to quell Indian hostilities in the middle of the nineteenth century, its remaining five structures commemorate and celebrate the very item it was supposed to destroy—Indian folklore and culture.

The towns of Toppenish and White Swan host an annual Indian powwow and rodeo during the first week of July. It features dances, traditional games, and a memorial for tribal ancestors.

Continuing north along I-82 the traveler reaches the agriculture capital, Yakima. This town and its surrounding valley feature tower-

Vibrant color begins to appear **above left** in early spring all along the river, and by mid-summer entire banks disappear under blooms.

Delicate blossoms **above right** populate a 34 acre wildflower preserve along the Oregon rim of the Columbia River Gorge.

Stepped, treeless plateaus **below** make a slow march down the Columbia at The Dalles—an arid landscape.

The improbable Regency-style edifice of Maryhill **overleaf**, perched on a hill overlooking the Columbia, houses a remarkable Impressionist art collection. **133**

The splendid summits of the Cascades **above** loom above Che Elum in the Snoqualmie National Forest.

The rapid building of **the railroad network** across the continent stimulated a great westward migration after the Civil War. By 1890 the 'last frontier' had disappeared.

A cowboy **right** tries to maintain his seat on an enraged bull. Apart from a one-handed death grip, the cowboy needs an aggressive will (what one taciturn contestant describes as "positive mental attitude"). Unlike horses, which have the good grace to walk away from a downed rider, bulls ascribe to the "don't get mad, get even" theory and seem to enjoy trampling and goring fallen cowboys.

ing Cascades on its west side and the quilted pattern of orchards, hopyards, and vineyards in all other directions. Three hundred days of sunshine annually are a great help, too. Numerous farmer's markets and the Central Washington State Fair held each September are testimony to the area's prominence in apple, mint, and hops production. West of town, in the Snoqualmie National Forest, one can backpack and ski at White Pass Village. In town the Yakima Valley Museum features a section dedicated to its favorite son, the late Justice William O. Douglas. A festive Cinco de Mayo is held in Yakima in honor of the area's sizable Spanish-speaking population, and several rodeos are held in the month of July—as befits its Western image.

Both the Yakima and the Tieton rivers offer river-rafting adventures and trout-fishing in abundance. During the salmon season at several dams along the Yakima River you can still see Indians fishing with dip-net technique—a traditional and very effective (and very controversial) method.

North of Yakima is the Yakima River Canyon with its narrow 36-mile gorge. Rock-hounds can search for petrified wood while canoeists quietly explore the river. Springtime brings forth an amazing display of delicate wildflowers along the rim of the gorge.

Farther north along US 97 is the town of Ellensburg, which once gloried in the name "Robbers' Roost." Ellensburg now claims special recognition as the exact center of the state of Washington. Although this claim is unlikely to draw many visitors, the town does have other attributes. The arrival of the Northern Pacific Railroad in 1886 inaugurated Ellensburg's boom days, still visible in its late nineteenth-century buildings. On Labor Day weekend Ellensburg hosts its annual rodeo and Kittitas County Fair. If you've climbed every mountain and are feeling blasé about this world's challenges, enter your name in the wild cow-milking contest. You'll gain new respect for the gentle bovine.

East of Ellensburg, near the town of Vantage, is Ginkgo Petrified State Park. Petrified logs lie strewn about in mute testimony to the actions of ancient lakes. Just south of Vantage at Wanapum Dam on the Columbia, visitors get a panoramic view of the river.

North of Ellensburg lies Wenatchee, the self-proclaimed "Apple Capital of the World." The town enjoys an enviable position on the Columbia River, next door to the Wenatchee National Forest and the east slopes of the Cascades. Hay fever sufferers should avoid this area in the spring as hillsides explode in clouds of white apple blossoms. Not only does

Wenatchee produce and ship more apples than any other region in the world, it also is no slouch in the production of prunes, peaches, pears, and apricots. The Washington State Apple Blossom Festival is an annual rite of spring here.

East of Wenatchee is the Wenatchee National Forest, which extends from the Yakima Nation Indian Reservation north along the Columbia River Basin to the Lake Chelan National Recreational Area. The Pacific Crest Trail follows the western boundary line from Goat Rocks Wilderness in the south to the Glacier Peak Wilderness in the north.

Lake Chelan

Bordering on the eastern fringe of the National Forest and almost directly north from Wenatchee is the little town of Chelan. Chelan's claim to fame is its position on the southeastern tip of the lake of the same name; it is the focus of much of the recreational diversity of the region. Lake Chelan's southeastern tip, nestled in the warm, dry climate of central Washington, makes it one of the state's leading water recreation areas. When everywhere else is rained out, vacationers can sail Lake Chelan's crystal waters, cruise its shoreline, or lie comatose on its sun-drenched beaches. Windsurfing, canoeing, waterskiing, and of course swimming and boating are a few of the popular activities.

But the best part of Lake Chelan is hidden beyond the reach of the Sunday driver. Knifing 55 miles into the heart of the Cascades, the fjordlike lake squeezes down in places to less than half a mile in width—at depths of nearly 1,500 feet. After Crater Lake, this body of water is the deepest in the Pacific Northwest. Penetrating into some of the area's most spectacular scenery, the upper part of the lake is accessible only by boat or floatplane (the latter operated daily by Chelan Airways). Roads extend uplake only as far as Twenty-five Mile Creek on the south side (about 25 miles northwest of the town of Chelan) and Manson on the north side (about eight miles from town). Several boat ramps are located around the southern edge of the lake for private boat launching, and there are several boat-only lakeside campgrounds dotting the shore.

Every summer morning (about four times the rest of the year), the *Lady of the Lake* departs Chelan for its nine-hour round trip up to Stehekin and back. By midlake, Chelan begins to be real wilderness as the mountain walls squeeze in on either side. Dense stands of pines grow right to the water's edge interspersed with sheer rock walls and spindly waterfalls. The vertical scale is no illusion—Chelan is the deepest gorge in North America (8,500 feet from lake bottom to ridge crest).

The tiny, isolated community of Stehekin, with its fifty inhabitants at the farthest reach of the lake, is a comfortable resting point. A rustic lodge and cabins provide overnight accommodations, but most passengers either return to Chelan the same day or use Stehekin as their starting point for cross-country treks. The Stehekin River Trail just north of the settlement is a southern gateway to the North Cascades National Park.

Plunging 55 miles into the heart of the Cascades, the chill waters of Lake Chelan **left** are flanked by snow-dusted peaks.

Forget about Johnny Appleseed, pomology—the science of fruit cultivation—is a difficult occupation. Tidy rows of apple orchards **far left** nestle up against the hills in Leavenworth, Washington.

137

GHOST TOWNS

Ghost towns are of special interest to history buffs seeking the old towns and atmosphere of the gold rush and settler days. The towns and their brief histories listed below are in varying stages of abandonment and decay; some are still sparsely inhabited. Some are fascinating for what still remains to be seen, others for their glorious and riproaring past. All are evocative of the Old West, and any visitor with imagination can picture the exuberance of these once thriving communities on the edge of the frontier, home to trappers, saloonkeepers, shop owners, loggers, occasionally a minister, usually farmers, and always miners.

Directions to some of the ghost towns are difficult, if not impossible, to give. In those cases, travelers should locate topographic maps for particular locations. Most libraries have complete sets of these maps, or they may be purchased through retailers or from the United States Geological Survey office. The Denver section of the USGS has for sale all maps covering the western United States. Should you wish to contact them, their address is: Denver Distribution Section, U.S. Geological Survey, Denver Federal Center, Building 41, Denver, CO 80225. Visitors should inquire at the nearest ranger station or town about the availability and quality of drinking water in the ghost towns. Since many of the wells are from the gold-boom era, they may contain arsenic from the mining operations, or various other metals that should not be consumed. Also be aware that many of the houses, buildings, and/or entire towns are now owned by private parties and the property belongs to them. Bear in mind too that the following is by no means an exhaustive or complete listing.

Barkerville British Columbia

Located fifty-nine miles east of Quesnel. Of all the ghost towns scattered among the hills and valleys of the Pacific Northwest, Barkerville is possibly the best known and certainly one of the better restored. Situated in the midst of the Cariboo gold country, nineteenth-century Barkerville was reputedly the largest city west of Chicago and north of San Francisco. Known as the "Gold Capital of the World" the town

At the height of British Columbia's gold rush in the mid-nineteenth century, the thriving metropolis of Barkerville epitomized "civilization." Its inhabitants liked to compare their town to San Francisco and Chicago. Among Barkerville's many facilities were several churches, a court house **opposite**, and Kelly's well-stocked General Store **right**. The town burned to the ground in 1868 and its halcyon days came to an end.

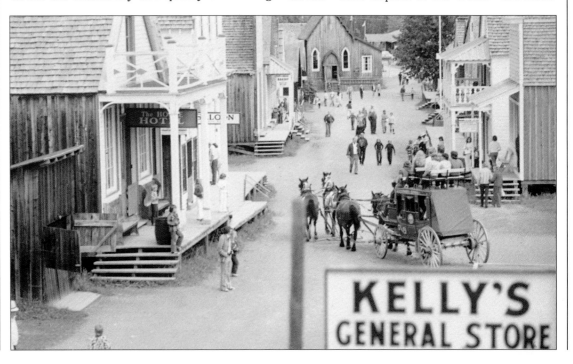

KELLY'S GENERAL STORE

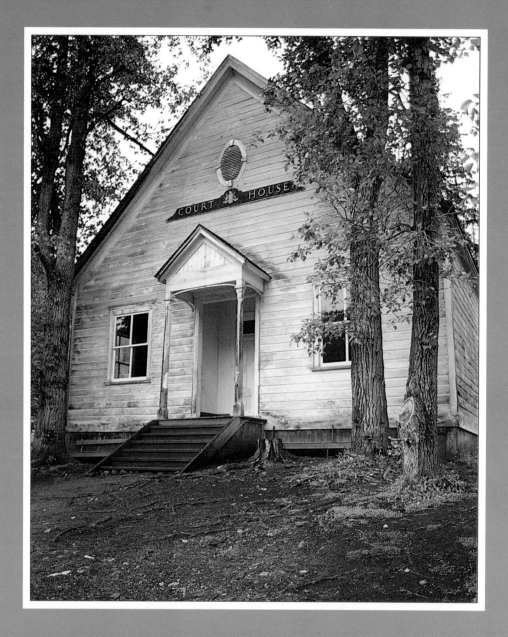

One of the many buildings that has been restored in Barkerville is this fine church shown here with citizens of the town in contemporary costume.

thrived in its heyday from 1869 to 1885.

Billy Barker was a Cornish seaman who struck it rich in 1862 beside Williams Creek. When news of his phenomenal strike got out other fortune hunters hurried to his camp and the town of Barkerville grew up almost overnight. With only one muddy street the town was hardly the parallel of San Francisco or Chicago, to which it freely compared itself, but it lacked few services. Banks, a blacksmith, stores, saloons, hotels, churches, butchers, and a sizable Chinatown were in some of the many buildings that have been restored to their former glory. The town also boasted a troupe of "Hurdy Gurdy" girls—German women of dubious repute who danced in the saloons to an instrument known as the hurdy gurdy. At the height of its activity 10,000 souls inhabited Barkerville before a disastrous fire gutted the town in the fall of 1868. Although quickly rebuilt, Barkerville's glory days were finished as the gold ran out and miners decamped for more profitable fields. Barker himself, having successfully drunk his fortune, died penniless and alone in an old folks' home in Victoria in 1894.

Restoration of the town began in 1958. Today, in addition to the reconstructed buildings on the site, there are a large number of displays and various summer activities used to depict the life-styles and working methods of the pioneer miners and townspeople.

Granite City, British Columbia

Located 12 miles from Princeton. When a man, aptly named John Chance, decided to try a little-used Indian trail as a shortcut, he stumbled upon a small tributary of the Tulameen and Similkameen rivers. Like many of his time, Chance was unable to pass a body of flowing water without panning for gold. This nondescript stream, later named Granite Creek, yielded pan after pan of gold on that July day of 1885. Chance hurried into the nearest town to register his claim. Despite his efforts at secrecy, word inevitably got out, and

prospectors began pouring into the area as the yield of the Cariboo and East Kootenay river further to the north declined.

This once booming town was, in its halcyon days, considered to be the third-largest settlement in British Columbia. Log cabins and tents lining the three streets parallel to the stream were the earliest town. No fewer than a dozen saloons, nine grocery stores, two jewelers, a drug store, and a shoemaker did flourishing trade as gold and platinum (the latter considered useless by most miners at the time!) were pulled daily from nearby claims.

Neither the source nor any substantial lode was ever discovered, and as the gold began to pan out, so people moved on to richer claims. A short fifteen years after Chance made his discovery Granite City was truly a ghost town. By 1900 the streams and creeks had been totally mined of their shallow gold. Most of the original buildings disappeared after fire twice swept the town, but a few buildings remain in advanced stages of decay to bear witness to the once-thriving community. A cairn now marks the site of Chance's discovery.

Fort Steele, British Columbia

Located ten miles northeast of Cranbrook on Highway 93-95. Originally known as "Galbraith's Ferry," Fort Steele became in 1887 the first headquarters in British Columbia of the Royal Canadian Mounted Police. The Mounties had been formed to bring law and order to the uproarious goldfields of nineteenth-century British Columbia. When the Mounties left the following year, the town was renamed for their R.C.M.P. superintendent, Samuel B. Steele.

When the railway came through in 1889, bypassing Fort Steele in favor of Cranbrook to the south, the population of the town began to decrease as businesses and government offices moved to Cranbrook. The first decade of this century found Fort Steele a true ghost town, and by 1948 the buildings were in an advanced state of decay. In 1969 the province

On the perimeter of abandoned Fort Steele **above**, children relive the wild-west gold-rush days of British Columbia.

decided to restore the site to represent East Kootenay life-styles of 1890–1905. Today the site has over forty reconstructed buildings, including the original Mounties buildings, and famous Clydesdale horses, steam locomotives, farm machinery, and a museum. Pioneer crafts and life-styles are demonstrated during the summer months, and there are lectures and sleigh rides in the winter.

An administrative center for the region, Fort Steele was never one of the boistrous miners' towns that most ghost towns represent. However, an interesting cemetery nearby contains many prospectors' graves.

Ashcroft Manor British Columbia

Located just off the Cariboo Highway near Cache Creek. Not actually a town or even a ghost town, nevertheless Ashcroft Manor is still fascinating for its history and its personalities. Two English brothers, Henry and Clement Cornwall, developed Ashcroft Manor on the road to Barkerville as an inn for the weary overlanders. In time-honored British fashion the two brothers did their utmost to import into the pagan colony all the best traditions of English country living—foxhunting being foremost among these. Hounds and horses were imported from England and the coyote was steadfastly referred to as the "fox." The hotel, built of stout logs, still stands and still welcomes guests.

Skamokawa Washington

Located six miles west of Cathlamet on SR 4. This was the site of an Indian village over 2,000 years ago. Skamokawa (Skum-MAH-kuh-way) is an Indian word meaning "smoke over the water," referring to the morning fog at the confluence of Skamokawa Creek and the Columbia River. Skamokawa is also the name of the last chief of the Wahkiakum Indians, who sold this land to the federal government in 1851. The first white settlement was established here in 1844 with the development of logging, commercial salmon-fishing, and dairy-farming. Its boom period took place between 1880 and 1910 when the town had a hotel, shipyard, cannery, hall, two churches, two saloons, two butchers, two real estate agents, a carpenter, cooper, notary public, barber, and three large shingle mills. Skamokawa also had the first cooperative creamery in the state that specialized in the making of sweet butter.

The town's decline began with the Depression, when natural resource-based industries were hard hit. Once known as "little Venice" because the creek was the town's main thoroughfare, the building of the Ocean Beach Highway through Skamokawa in 1933 changed the focus and destroyed some of the charm of the town. The creamery was sold in 1943 and soon closed.

Remnants of this little Columbia River town still remain. The neighborhoods still retain their picturesque names such as Swedetown, Sleepy Hollow, Moe Hill, and Missouri Flats. The area is scenic and good for bicycling. Canoeing on the creek is pleasant on a summer day and nearby is the Columbia White Trail Deer National Wildlife Refuge.

Ruby, Washington

Located on the eastern edge of the Olympic Peninsula, just north of SR 16. This was one of the earliest and most important lumber-producing centers on the Pacific coast. Still an active sawmill town, it was built in the nineteenth century as a company town. Still standing are some Greek Revival cottages, New England boxlike houses, Victorian homes, a church, community center, and company general store built in 1853. Pope and Talbot company employees still live here, and the town is being restored to its earlier nineteenth-century look. Of special interest is the Walker Ames House, which was the home of the first mill manager, with a panoramic view of the mill.

Jacksonville, Oregon

Although not technically a ghost town, Jacksonville, located on SR 238, became the Oregon Territory's first boom town in 1852 with the discovery of gold in nearby creeks. Now restored and rebuilt, the town has about eighty buildings to explore including a bank that handled more than $30 million in gold in its day, three churches, and a hotel built in the 1860s. The cemetery, where several prospectors are buried, is interesting. You can also try your luck panning for gold on the eastern edge of town.

Granite, Oregon

Located fifteen miles west of Sumpter on Highway 220. Granite was once the smallest incorporated town in the United States, with a population of one! There are a number of old buildings dating from the 1800's (the town grew, subsequent to its incorporation), and the main street still gives the impression of nineteenth-century life with its false-fronted stores. The current population of Granite is approximately twenty souls.

Hardman, Oregon

Located off Highway 207. Hardman came into being because of a bitter rivalry between the towns of Raw Dog and Yellow Dog. Both wanted a post office, but only one could have it because of their respective sizes. It was determined that Raw Dog had several more inhabitants, so everyone moved to Raw Dog from Yellow Dog. The surrounding population decided that since the new town was comprised of dogs, it should be called Dog Town, and the name stuck until the government, thinking the name Dog Town a trifle undignified for a United States Post Office, changed the name. There are many old buildings and a very interesting cemetery still to inspect.

Fort Steele **left**, huddled against a backdrop of glowering mountains, was the first administrative headquarters of the Mounties in British Columbia. Reconstructed in 1969, Fort Steele is today a living museum **below** depicting East Kootenay lifestyles.

THE CASCADES

The majestic **bald eagle**, with its distinctive white head and tail, has a wingspread of up to eight feet. It lives near rivers and lakes and feeds mainly on fish.

he Cascades, running for 600 miles from northern California up into British Columbia, form the backbone of the Pacific Northwest. Broken only once by the Columbia River Gorge, this backbone includes hundreds of lakes, nearly a thousand glaciers, towering peaks, huge national forests, and at least one erupting volcano. A spectacular natural playground, these mountains are dotted with county, state, and federal parks providing ready access to boating, fishing, skiing, camping, climbing, and hiking. The Pacific Crest Trail, running the length of the Cascades, is the main hiking thoroughfare in a vast network of winding trials. It need hardly be added that the Cascades form one of this region's most valuable recreational areas.

To the west of the range the moisture-laden Pacific currents drop their dampness, feeding lush forests and tumbling rivers. To the east open pine forests meet sun-drenched plains and desert-rock outcrops. Trappers from the Hudson's Bay Company and North West Company were undoubtedly the first white men to explore these jagged peaks. But it was Lewis and Clark who gave us our first description: "Down these heights frequently descend the most beautiful cascades, one of which a large creek, throws itself over a perpendicular rock 300 feet above the water, while other smaller streams precipitate themselves from a still greater elevation." Indeed, it is believed that the name of this range derives from these numerous waterfalls issuing from the mountains—the Cascades.

On the southern end of Oregon's Cascade range is the state's largest natural freshwater lake: Upper Klamath Lake, with the sizable town of Klamath Falls at its southern tip. The Klamath Basin area also serves as an important wildlife refuge: more than 250 species of birds, including the greatest wintering population of bald eagles, have been sighted in this Pacific flyway area.

Dozens of high alpine lakes dot the area around Mount McLoughlin providing superb fishing, waterskiing, and boating. Hunters can stalk the marshes and forests for geese, ducks, and deer. Winter brings snowmobiling, ice-skating, ice-fishing, and ice-climbing to this lake country. Pelican Butte, 35 miles northwest of Klamath Falls, offers uncrowded alpine skiing with miles of cross-country ski trails.

Klamath Lake **right** is the largest of several high-altitude lakes surrounding Mount McLoughlin in Oregon's southern Cascades.

Opposite A tug nudges logs into a "raft" for towing to a nearby sawmill at Lumas, Washington.

Wizard Island **right**, the islet in the middle of Crater Lake, is actually a volcano within a volcano.

As a test of courage, Indian braves used to clamber down the treacherous lava cliffs of Oregon's Crater Lake **below**. Survivors bathed in the chilling lake.

Crater Lake

Alpine-clear water tumbles over the rocks **left** of Vidae Falls in Crater Lake National Park, southern Oregon.

Crater Lake, snuggled into the very crest of the Cascade Range in the Rogue River National Forest, is a spectacular testament to volcanic power. A caldera, formed when the ancient is 12,000-foot Mount Mazama collapsed 6,000 years ago, this lake is six miles long and four and a half miles wide, reaching a depth of 1,962 feet. Steep lava cliffs rise to 2,000 feet above the lake. In the summer visitors can explore along the paved 33-mile rim or take a two-hour boat trip around the lake. Despite an annual snowfall of 50 feet the park is open in the winter, and visitors on snowshoes or cross-country skis can explore the pristine stillness of the snow-rimmed lake.

Elsewhere in the Rogue River Natonal Forest, fishing sites abound, The forest is easily reached from Medford to the west or Klamath Falls on the southern end. The Umpqua National Forest borders Crater Lake and has its own year-round Diamond Lake recreation area in the shadow of 9,182-foot Mount Thielsen.

In the Deschutes National Forest, the perpetually snow-clad Three Sisters dominate the skyline. Each over 10,000 feet, these cones are all that remain of another ancient volcano's rim. On nearby Mount Bachelor is one of the west's premier ski developments. For a driving tour through one of North America's most beautiful alpine lake basins the Cascade Lakes Highway is a must on any itinerary. The loop drive leads west into the range from Bend and also provides access to the Three Sisters Wilderness.

Three major peaks tower above the Willamette National Forest: 10,495-foot Mount Jefferson, Three Fingered Jack (7,841 feet), and Mount Washington, 7,800 feet. All three offer challenging climbing routes if your death wish is fairly strong. The McKenzie Pass area presents unforgettable volcanic terrain crossed by SR 126 from Eugene.

In Oregon's northernmost Cascade region is the granddaddy of the state's peaks, 11,245-foot Mount Hood. Just a half hour's drive from Portland (and presenting a magnificent view

Three Sisters Mountains sit on the horizon **right**, each wearing her year-round dress of snow. All over 10,000 feet, these mountains protect a dense wilderness said to be home to the legendary Bigfoot.

Wierdly shaped spires **right** jab the sky at Pinnacles near the eastern border of Crater Lake National Park.

to the city of its snow-capped peak), Mount Hood supports a year-round ski area at historic Timberline Lodge. And Oregon's northern Cascades have plenty of recreational possibilities. Sliders on Alpine grass sleds replace skiers from June through October at Government Camp. The Clackamas River offers ideal fishing and white-water thrills. Forest Service roads give access to remote campgrounds, hot springs and stream and lake fishing sites too numerous to enumerate. An especially picturesque and historic drive is Highway 26 looping from Portland through Barlow Pass to the Columbia at the town of Hood River and back again to Portland. Barlow Pass was built in 1846 by the enterprising Samuel Barlow of Illinois as an alternative to the treacherous float trip through the Columbia River Gorge. After its tortuous construction this road became the standard immigrant route into the Willamette Valley, and Barlow was allowed to charge a toll for his trouble. (One pioneer, unhappy at what he considered an extortionate toll, declared Barlow "the meanest man in all of the Oregon country.")

The Cascades in Washington

Continuing north across the Columbia is the first of Washington's several forests in the Cascades, the Gifford Pinchot National Forest. In fact, two of Washington's three national parks are in the Cascades: Mount Rainier National Park and the newly created North Cascades National Park. There are several national recreational areas and officially designated wilderness regions offering plenty of room to roam amidst the spectacular scenery and wide-open country.

Four major and two minor highways cross the rocky spine of the Cascades in Washington, providing comfortable access to the beauty of these mountains. In the spring and early summer, wildflowers blossom forth in mountain meadows and streams rise high with snow melt. Alpine meadows around Chinook Pass are especially rewarding for their early summer wildflowers. In summer the heady fragrance of evergreens permeates as outdoor enthusiasts flock to the campgrounds, hiking trails, and white-water river runs. The bright foliage of fall—vine and big leaf maple, sumac and larch—set's the mountainsides ablaze with color. Both Chinook Pass and White Pass in Mount Rainier National Park have outstanding fall color displays. Three of the cross-Cascades routes are open all winter for skiing, ideal for downhill, cross-country, and snowshoeing. Five major volcanic mountains punctuate the skyline of the Washington Cascades, and the most famous of these is Mount St. Helens, the first peak you see as you drive north from Portland.

Just to the east of Mount St. Helens is the snowy bulk of Mount Adams (12,276 feet), the bereaved lover in Indian legend of the beautiful Mount St. Helens. Alpine meadows, lakes, and relatively open country combine to create an area of primitive beauty. Fishing, boating, hiking, and camping are popular activities in this area. For thrill seekers, ice caves are plentiful on Mount Adams. Some have openings allowing admittance down a ladder for close-at-hand inspection of the bizarre formations in the cave. For the nervous, however, it will not help you to know that these caves usually have other, deeper caves and sometimes even open chasms beneath them

A 33-mile rim drive skirts the
edge of Oregon's Crater Lake, providing
spectacular views into the caldera
of the ancient volcano Mount Mazama.

Tawny fall colors line a turbulent stream in the Cascades **right**.

An assiduous waterfall **above left** carves its way through densely forested slopes in Mount Rainier National Park.

Bristling crags of Liberty Bell Mountain **left** lie stripped of snow in northern Washington.

(making the ice floor seem like, well, thin ice ...) The Mount Adams Wilderness area is trespassed only by the Pacific Crest Trail.

Mount Rainier

Next along the Cascade range is Mount Rainier, visible from Puget Sound as it rises majestically to its grand height of 14,410 feet. An excellent access road from the south, US 12 leads east from I-5 past two big water recreation lakes through the old logging communities of Morton, Randle, and Packwood at the southern entrance of Mount Rainier National Park. To celebrate its Paul Bunyan traditions the little town of Morton holds its annual "Loggers Jubilee" when 'misery whips" are unpacked and loggers of today try the methods and tools of the old days. While in Morton, the Tilton and Cowlitz rivers are excellent steelhead streams. US 12 continues up to the 4,500-foot summit of White Pass—a top-rated ski area—and descends along the Tieton River, past prime camping and water recreation areas finishing in the wheat fields of Yakima on the eastern edge of the Cascades.

Just south of White Pass is the Goat Rocks Wilderness area, home to elk, pikas, marmots, and mountain goats. This area is rewarding for hikers and backpackers, and several outfitters in the vicinity organize horse-pack trips.

On the north side of Mount Rainier National Park SR 410 follows the White River through the magnificent stands of virgin timber in Federation Forest, then climbs past Crystal Mountain Ski Area to 4,630-foot Cayuse Pass. The last few miles before you reach the summit give you dramatic close-up views of the glacier-clad north and east faces of Mount Rainier. SR 410 then climbs to 5,400-foot Chinook Pass (closed in winter) before descending along the American River to US 12 and Yakima.

Two major roads, I-90 and US 2 (or a combination of the two), provide easy access to the alpine beauty of the central Cascades. Washington's major cross-mountain highway, I-90, runs from Seattle to Ellensburg via the lowest of the passes, 3,022-foot Snoqualmie. Four ski facilities at the summit form the state's largest ski area. One, Alpental, is open in the summer for hiking. The Pacific Crest Trail passes over the summit heading north along the borders of the Wenatchee and Snoqualmie National Alpine Wilderness.

It is worth taking a short side trip north of Ellensbury along local roads to the small towns of upper Kittitas County. Just on the edge

Wildflowers nestle in the precarious soil of Rampart Ridge **center** overlooking alpine lakes in Washington.

of Wenatchee National Forest the towns of Cle Elum, Roslyn, Ronald, and Easton were the center of a coal-mining area opened in 1886. The largest of these four is Cle Elum, Indian for "swift water." And the "swift water" is the Yakima River as it descends from Lake Cle Elum, a fine fishing lake seven miles northeast of town. Cle Elum is also a good spot to find outfitters for canoeing and rafting trips down the river. The minuscule settlement of Liberty, tucked away into the hills, was once the center of the gold-mining region east of Lake Cle Elum. Now it is a historic district, where visitors can watch gold-panning demonstrations. The hills around this area abound in clues to its past: abandoned mine shafts, tailings, and long-forgotten ghost towns.

Continuing north, the next east-west route across the Cascades is US 2, which follows the Skykomish River eastward from Everett to Wenatchee through a handful of little logging towns to crest at Stevens Pass (4,061 feet), another major ski area. The Burlington Northern Railroad follows the same route and plunges beneath the pass through Cascade Tunnel which, at nearly eight miles in length, is the longest in the western hemisphere. The east side of Stevens Pass is the best for sightseeing. As it follows the Wenatchee River (a major rafting river) into Leavenworth, the highway cuts through Tumwater Canyon, a narrow rocky gorge with lovely views. Fall foliage here is some of the best in the state.

The little town of Leavenworth, nestled in the foothills of the Cascades' eastern slopes, was once a forgotten railroad town. However, it has revived itself by adopting a Bavarian theme complete with gingerbread buildings, European restaurants, lots of flowers, and more German music than you can probably stand. The May Festival—a traditional Bavarian celebration of the awakening of spring—is a big event here. Lake Wenatchee, just to the north of Leavenworth, is a prime water-recreation area.

The high mountain slopes of Mount Baker, just on the western border of the North Cascades National Park, are accessible from Bellingham on SR 542. If you are sick of the rat race, rush to the North Cascades, because here, in virtually untouched wilderness, you can really escape civilization. It is an area of glaciers, rock-climbing, and ski-touring where you may still encounter black bears blissfully

The **sugar pine** gets its name from the sugary resin that exudes from its trunk when it is cut. It is the tallest of pines, growing to over 200 feet, and has the **154** largest cones.

snacking on wild berries in the summer. Here tall fir and spruce stand beneath jagged peaks and alongside plunging waterfalls. East along the Skagit River (noted for its bald eagles in winter and white-tailed deer all year round) the highway winds past many small towns to Newhalem, headquarters for Seattle City Light's three-dam hydroelectric complex.

At Washington Pass (5,477 feet) there is an overlook that gives you stunning views of the valley of the Methow River, full of abandoned mines and ghost towns. Fall color displays are excellent, particularly the yellow larch standing out against the dark evergreens.

Just east of the Washington Pass area on SR 20 is the little town of Winthrop, another restored pioneer mining village. The Old West spirit has been recaptured in its carefully reconstructed main street: false-fronted buildings, wooden sidewalks, and old-fashioned streetlights are reminiscent of the 1890s, when a mining boom attracted many settlers to this area. Continuing on SR 20, past Winthrop, is the little town that delights in the name of Twisp. Twisp is the home base of the

Towering over all its companions, Mount Rainier **above** is Washington's mightiest peak. The monarch soars to 14,410 feet and can be seen from Seattle.

The snow-mantled massif of Mount Adams **left** backdrops a quiet, open meadow in Washington's Cascades range.

Industrious little logging communities **overleaf** dot its lower flanks, holding annual "loggers' jubilees" to celebrate their Paul Bunyan traditions. **155**

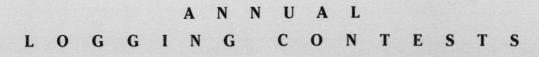

A tree feller rests his saw on a stump **above** during
a timber harvest.
Using a wedge and an axe, a contestant **center left**
in a speed-chopping event "beavers" his way through a log.
Loggers in Morton, in Mount Rainier National Park
below left, pit their strength against logs—in a timed event.
A lumberjack adjusts his "spurs"—really a belt **below
right**. This belt, plus steel climbers on the soles of his boots, will
enable him to "climb" the trunk of the 100-foot tree.

North Cascades Smoke Jumpers, and visitors may tour the base, including its parachute loft, fire-fighting equipment, and aircraft. It is also possible to watch the practice jumps during early June training sessions. Visitors learn at first hand how a possibly devastating fire can be contained in virtually unpenetrated terrain. Smoke jumpers definitely have the right stuff.

Logging

The numerous logging shows in the Pacific Northwest reflect the continuing importance of this industry to the area. Wherever there is big timber these competitions test the ordinary working skills of lumberjacks: strength, speed, and agility. In the old days logging contests provided entertainment to the men in their remote forest camps. Now the competitions have been brought to nearby towns and are no less thrilling to watch.

The sawdust, sweat, and deafening whine

of saws tell you this is for "real" men—these guys do not eat quiche. You will see "buckers" power one- and two-person handsaws, called "misery whips," through huge logs in timed events. Or how about a logger free-swinging with an axe, chopping through the very log on which he's standing? And then there are the real "he-men" who pitch their double-bitted axes into four-inch targets at twenty paces.

But if all this raises a yawn there are still the

One good way for refugees from the "real" world to unwind **top** is a float trip on the Yakima (near Ellensburg).

These densely packed Douglas firs **left** represent 15 years of growth on a forestry plantation in Washington.

Lake Wenatchee **below** is a resort area for all seasons: skiing in winter, hiking in spring, summer and fall. Fishing, hunting and climbing are also popular, or you can simply stand back and admire the gorgeous scenery.

Brilliant fall foliage skirts the
banks of a mountain stream in Tumwater
Canyon.

Bavarian folk-dancers **above left** swirl in a lively celebration of the May Festival—the awakening of spring—held annually in Leavenworth.

Rubber-tired skidders **above right** are normally used to move the logs—up to 18 at a time—to an assembly point.

The familiar logging truck **below**. Sturdy it is, but maddeningly slow if you've ever had the misfortunate to be stuck behind a laden one on a winding two-lane mountain road.

speed-climbing and tree-topping contests. In each timed event the lumberjack must climb a one hundred-foot tree using belt and steel climbers on his boots. In the speed climb, he hits a bell at the top of the tree and then drops to the ground, casually covering twenty feet in each downward leap. In the tree-topping event, the logger cuts a slice from the top of the tree with a chain saw before descending in similar fashion.

For comic relief there is the log-rolling event in which two (or more) loggers try to dump each other from a bobbing log into a pond. Other events include skidder races, horse- and oxen-pulling contests, and tests of logging-truck driving skills. And of course there's always the World Championship Riding Lawnmower Race held each year in Morton, Washington. The skills tested in this last event seems to be in an inverse relationship between amount of alcohol consumed and fixed gaze direction.

This autumn scene on the south fork of the Skokomish River **above** shows the total effect of clear-cut silviculture.

When forest-floor clearance is tight, large balloons **below** will be used to haul logs out of remote areas like the Hoh River in Washington's Olympic Peninsula.

Timber Harvesting

Although the Indians felled the few trees they required for their dwellings and canoes, the Spanish Franciscans led by Father Junipero Serra were the first to cut timber on a large scale in the Pacific Northwest. Lumbering has been vital to the development of the west since the latter half of the nineteenth century. At that time it provided employment and building materials as well as bringing in much-needed capital, as the area's number-one export, for development of the region. The market grew and so did the need for cheap labor; Chinese workers were imported to work in the forests from northern California to British Columbia. Many of these workers remained in the Pacific Northwest, adding a new flavor to the ethnic makeup of the area. Oregon now claims to be the leading timber-producing state, with 20 percent of the country's total timber growing within its boundaries. But the oldest continually active sawmill in the United States is in Port Gamble, Washington—a company town built in 1854 for the Puget Mill Company and still running today.

The first step in timber-harvesting occurs at the very earliest sign of spring when the snows have just begun to melt. A lumber company surveyor goes into the forest to mark the trees to be cut, selecting those trees that have reached their greatest growth. Next, the loggers move in, finding the marked trees. After first deciding which direction the tree should fall they make an undercut on the "fall" side, cutting partially through the trunk. A second cut is started above the first and slanted downward. When this wedge-shaped section is later removed from the trunk the tree leans over it. Incidentally, the motor-driven "gang saw" or "sash gang" saw used by loggers today is a modern version of the first Roman-engineered handsaws built in 1500 B.C.

The loggers then move to the opposite side of the tree to make the back cut, placing it a little higher than the undercut. If the tree "settles" its weight onto the saw chain at this point the men force wooden wedges into the

cut to "lift" the trunk and force a wider opening. It is at this very critical point that the undercut is removed by imbedding an axe head into the wedge and jerking it away. If the tree doesn't fall, more wedges are driven into its back cut until the tree is forced over and falls.

Once the tree has fallen (and the dust clears) the "buckers" move in to saw the giant trunks into a standard 32-foot length, simultaneously removing the branches. The "skidders" then move the logs, usually two to eight at a time depending on the forest-floor clearance, to an assembly point. The logs are then moved to their final destination at a nearby sawmill, either on the laboriously slow logging truck (you may have the misfortune to be stuck behind one on a winding mountain road) or as part of a chained log raft moving down a river. Once the logs reach the mills they are processed into lumber or paper products and readied for shipment around the world.

The abundant forest **above** — the Tacoma Narroms sawmill.

With vast stands of timber **below** throughout the area, forestry and the Pacific Northwest go hand-in-hand. These two lonely sentinels stand watch over a wintry landscape in Mount Rainier National Park.

163

PUGET SOUND

*P*uget Sound is a maritime world characterized by deep, protected harbors, tiny coves, inlets, and waterways bustling with all kinds of activity from oceangoing freighters to bathtub-sized pleasure craft. Puget Sound, an inland sea, is linked to the Pacific Ocean by the Strait of Juan de Fuca. Surrounding it are the major cities of Washington interspersed with tranquil farms, coastal forests, and small villages. From its southern reach at the state capital, Olympia, to the Strait of Juan de Fuca it is just 90 miles in length. Officially, Puget Sound terminates at the Hood Canal and the San Juan Islands are not part of it, but most Washingtonians consider the 172 islands of the San Juan group part of the sound. The islands themselves offer uninterrupted tranquility—some are heavily forested, uninhabited but for the occasional fisherman; others are patterned by tidy farms and villages that beg for the use of the overworked adjective "quaint." It is a pristine region of shimmering water against a backdrop of rich landscaping and white-mantled mountains. Perhaps that is why Puget Sound ranks near the top of Pacific Northwest vacation destinations.

The entire area had been explored and claimed for the Spanish crown by Bruno Heceta and Juan de Bodega y Quadra around 1775. And although it is disputed by historians, the Strait of Juan de Fuca is named for the Spanish navigator who probably first discovered it in 1592. The British had staked their claim earlier, however, some accounts asserting that Sir Francis Drake, in declaring "New Albion" British territory in 1579, meant everything north of San Francisco to the limit of his exploration—Vancouver Island. Captain James Cook's expedition in 1778, three years after Heceta's, missed both the mouth of the Columbia and the Strait of Juan de Fuca in the drizzle but went on to anchor in Friendly Cove on Vancouver Island's east coast. Cook sailed away with news that would change the fabric of Puget Sound's history: beaver pelts were in abundance and could be easily traded from the coastal Indians.

While British merchants piled the profitable fur trade by 1792, the British captain George Vancouver was busy exploring the inlets and bays of the Sound. Naming the Sound for one of his lieutenants on the voyage, Peter Puget, Vancouver went as far south as the present city of Tacoma. Today's explorers can see the same "lofty snow mountains and unnumerable pleasing landscapes" that delighted Vancouver and Puget.

First American Settlers

The first American settlers to Puget Sound founded the town of Tumwater at its very southern tip in 1845. As the California gold rush boomed, the demand for lumber to build homes and docks in the new city of San Francisco increased. The new settlement of Seattle, named for the hospitable chief of the Dwamish tribe, Chief Seathl, and the New England–style town of Port Gamble quickly became central ports in the west-coast lumber industry.

Although Americans were beginning to settle in the region, Puget Sound and most of the area south to the Columbia were, in reality, British-controlled through the presence of the Hudson's Bay Company at Fort Vancouver (on the Columbia) and Fort Nisqually (near Tacoma). America and Britain had agreed on a boundary at the 49th parallel, but the exact boundary placement was vague and mapmakers had arbitrarily bent the border to go between the islands in the Sound. Both sides claimed sunny San Juan Island. One June day in 1859 an American farmer caught a British pig in his potato patch and shot the offending animal. By the end of that summer American troops had fourteen cannons trained on British warships standing off Garrison Bay. Their two old posts, American Camp and English Camp, tell the story of this infamous standoff, still called the Pig War, perhaps because the pig was the only casualty.

Another humorous victim of the arbitrary 49th parallel is Point Roberts, a small town on the tip of a mainland peninsula jutting south into Puget Sound. The town of Point Roberts lies south of the 49th parallel and is American, but the mainland it is attached to is north and therefore Canadian. For the denizens of Point Roberts to shop in the nearest American town (Blaine) they must cross the border four times before returning home!

The ferry landing at Steilacoom **above** — Washington's oldest incorporated town, founded in 1854.

Many ferry boats—such as the M.V. *Coho*—ply the waters of Puget Sound **right**, bustling in and out of the cities lining the waterway. Port Angeles is home port for a major ferry service running between the Olympic Peninsula and Victoria, B.C.

Puget Sound Cities

Around Puget Sound are a variety of cities. Tacoma and Everett, old lumber towns, have grown to become major metropolitan areas. There is Olympia, the classically inspired state capital. Bremerton is home to a major naval shipyard and Bellevue is one gateway to the Cascades. In the very north is Bellingham, a recreational paradise and last major city before the Canadian border. Port Angeles, Oroville, and Anacortes are all Canadian gateways. And Seattle, founded on the lumber industry, dashed into the twentieth century on the crest of the Klondike gold rush and today offers cosmopolitan excitement mixed with a good dose of history.

Just above Olympia at the southern tip of the sound is Steilacoom, the first incorporated town of Washington Territory. This historical community has many firsts catering to both ends of the spectrum from saints to sinners: the first Protestant church and the first territorial jail.

Continuing northeast on I-5 is Tacoma, third largest of Washington's cities. Military history buffs should stop at the Fort Lewis Military Museum, one of the army's largest posts. Point Defiance Park, originally another military reservation, was acquired by the city in 1905. Its 700 acres offer wooded trails and beautiful rose gardens for city-weary travelers. The old Hudson's Bay Company's Fort Nisqually has been reconstructed and it houses an interesting museum. Those old enough to remember "Galloping Gertie"—an architectural folly nicknamed for the way the bridge swayed in the wind before collapsing in 1940—will want to visit the Narrows Bridge on the same site. One of the largest suspension bridges in the world, the Narrows Bridge does *not* sway as it links Tacoma to the Kitsap Peninsula.

On the peninsula is the navy town of Bremerton, home to the U.S. Pacific Fleet. These nval shipyards have hosted warships from the U.S.S. *Nebraska* to the Trident submarines. But none is more famous than the World War II battleship *Missouri*, now anchored here, veteran of Iwo Jima and Okinawa, and scene of the Japanese surrender.

Continuing north to Liberty Bay is Poulsbo, known as "little Norway" because of its early immigrants. This picturesque village retains an Old World charm, celebrating its Nordic heritage annually with a spring Viking Festival.

North of Poulsbo, where the Hood Canal meets Puget Sound, is Port Gamble. A historic

district, this was one of the earliest and most important lumber-producing centers on the Pacific. Still an active sawmill town, it exemplifies the mid-nineteenth-century company-owned town.

At the extreme northeast tip of the Olympic Peninsula, where it juts into the Strait of Juan de Fuca, is the historic town of Port Townsend, a jewel-box Victorian community suspended forever in the era of the 1890s. Once an active port, it is now a somewhat sleepy paper-mill town. The proliferation of fine old residences, buildings, forts, parks, and monuments earns it the reputation as the best example of a Victorian seacoast town north of San Francisco.

Just west of Port Townsend is the working city of Port Angeles, the northern gateway to the Olympic National Park and home to a ferry service operating the 18 miles across the Strait to Victoria, British Columbia.

Originally a military base, and acquired by the city in 1905, Port Defiance Park (seen here in an aerial view of Tacoma) **left** is a welcome green belt offering lovely gardens set amongst extensive hiking trails.

With Mount Rainier forming a majestic backdrop, the 605-foot Space Needle **below** thrusts skyward amongst the illuminations of Seattle.

This classic **Indian wooden mask** was painted and decorated with human hair by the Tsimshian tribe of British Columbia.

Seattle

Back on the mainland is Washington's premier city: Seattle. Christened in honor of Chief Seathl it is perhaps appropriate to begin the exploration of this gleaming city on the Sound by remembering its Indian antecedents. The Thomas Burke Museum on the University of Washington campus houses one of the country's finest collections of Northwest Indian art and culture. Nearby Tillicum Village is a kind of "living history" park showcasing native dances and artifacts (including a cedar longhouse), highlighted by a traditional baked salmon dinner, done Indian-style.

Settled relatively late, the city of Seattle did not really prosper until the middle of the nineteenth-century, when its fine protected harbor at Elliott Bay became a major maritime port. Today Seattle's waterfront is still a working port, home to shipbuilding, a sizable cargo port, public fishing, and a large ferry system. At Colman Dock you can learn the history of the "mosquito fleet," which operated from Seattle from 1860 to 1920. Out of some 500 steamers the sole remaining "mosquito" is the *Virginia V*, still plying the waters between Seattle and Poulsbo. Seattle is still a major port of call for ships bound for Alaska and the Orient, and two of its original shipments still dominate: wood products and fish.

Near the docks the Pike Place Public Market, begun in 1907, still brings local farmers and consumers face to face over fresh produce in the middle of this thriving city.

At the end of the nineteenth century Seattle was a boomtown, and Pioneer Square, near both Pike Place and the waterfront, was its heartbeat, complete with a real "skid road" down which huge logs were skidded into the sound for transport to nearby sawmills. As this young, brash city's fortunes boomed and eventually busted, Pioneer Square and its "skid road" were truly "on the skids." However, since its restoration in the 1960s Pioneer Square is once again the heartbeat of a delightful historic district. One of the more unusual tours in Seattle takes visitors underground. After a disastrous fire in 1889 the

streets around Pioneer Square were raised and the original levels left hollow. You can walk along musty corridors viewing deserted store fronts on this tour. Back aboveground, Capitol Hill is resplendent with mansions built by early Seattle money.

Another vital link in Seattle's industrial history is the Boeing Aircraft Company with its Pacific Museum of Flight at Boeing Field illustrating the history of the company. Many of Boeing's first aircraft were built in the famous "Red Barn" here.

Although Seattle is definitely still a working industrial city it is not without its requisite Pacific Northwest beauty. Look up: the city seems encircled by gleaming white peaks with the jagged Olympics to its west and the Cascades looming up in the east. Lake Washington is a popular spot for hiking trails with ample boating and fishing facilities as well. Mercer Island (named for one enterprising early Seattle resident, Asa Mercer) is also a relaxing greenbelt. Noting that the thriving export business in the nineteenth century was attracting more single men than single women, Mr. Mercer set out for the East to recruit eligible young ladies. Over the vocal disapproval of the Eastern press (notably *Harper's Weekly* and the New York *Herald*), he successfully recruited eleven spinsters on his first venture and Seattle lost eleven bachelors, including Asa Mercer himself.

Oldest of the Hudson's Bay Company posts on the Pacific Northwest coast, Fort Nisqually **above** displays the trim neatness typical of that efficient fur-trapping outfit.

Port Townsend **opposite**, in the northeast corner of the Olympic Peninsula, is a picturesque community that just begs for the adjective "quaint." Fine Victorian architecture, such as this small inn, rivals that of San Francisco for the same era.

One of the few open-air markets in the country **left**, Pike Place Market in Seattle is also one of the few remaining farmers' marts where fresh produce and seafood abound.

The Seattle Area

Short trips east of Seattle can be made to the towns of Carnation and Snoqualmie. Carnation is the home of the Carnation Research Farm, begun at the turn of the century, with the single purpose of breeding and developing superior dairy cows. Today's visitors can tour calf and maternity barns and the cow wash and see firsthand some very productive and contented cows.

Snoqualmie, on the western edge of Snoqualmie National Forest with its superb ski resorts, was named by local Indians for the supernatural powers of peace believed to be resident in a spectacular waterfall nearby. Today the falls have an underground power plant, surrounded by several nature trails in the park. The Puget Sound and Snoqualmie Valley Railroad operates a seven-mile round trip from Snoqualmie past the falls and south to North Bend.

Everett, lying north of Seattle on the sound, is developing into a major center for aircraft and shipbuilding industries: Boeing builds 747s here. Located at the mouth of the Snohomish River, the harbor of Everett has numerous ferries providing access to Whidbey Island. This is six miles south of Everett and is the longest island in Puget Sound. With the snow-capped Olympics as a backdrop this island of rolling pastures, thick forests, and acres of wild rhododendrons is a welcome respite from the industrialization of he mainland. Settled by Irish and Dutch immigrants, the marshy land has, over the years, been turned to profitable agriculture. At Greenbank is the largest loganberry farm in the United States. Driftwood-strewn sand and some of the best Dungeness crabbing are the attractions at Maxwelton, and grain and dairy cattle thrive here in the rainshadow of the Olympics. (Natives will cheerfully tell you their island gets "only" 17 inches a year, but it just so happens that in the winter this rain falls one day out of every two.)

Oak Harbor, largest of Whidbey's cities, is home to a modern defense installation, the navy's Tactical Electronic Warfare squadrons. Within close driving distance is an underwater state park for skin-diving enthusiasts. The navy calls this assignment the best-kept secret in the military.

North of Oak Harbor is a stunning example of modern engineering, the Deception Pass Bridge. Captain Vancouver believed Whidbey Island was part of the mainland; when he discovered a craggy gorge with currents of the sound rushing through, he named the passage

A ferry **right** boards Alaska-bound passengers at one of Seattle's several landings. The Kingdome in the background is home court for several of Seattle's professional sports teams.

Late afternoon sunlight filters onto Puget Sound **below**, bathing a ferry boat in autumnal shades.

"Deception." Salmon fishing is excellent nearby also.

Across the bridge is Fidalgo Island (named, as is Whidbey, for a member of Vancouver's crew), with the town of Anacortes located at its northern tip. Several ferry services operate from here to other points in the San Juan Islands as well as to Vancouver Island. Surely one of the more unusual tourist attractions in this early cannery town is the Women's Christian Temperance Union fountain in the center of town. Covering all possibilities, the fountain has drinking basins at varying heights for dogs, horses, and people. It is unclear whether or not the drinking fountain had much effect on the quite sizable saloon business in Anacortes (nor whether any dogs and horses were saved from evil drink). The highest point on Fidalgo is Mount Erie, and from its 1,270-foot summit you have an excellent view of the Olympic Peninsula and the Cascades with Mount Baker and Mount Rainier in fine relief. Six fresh water lakes surround the base of the mountain and provide excellent angling opportunities.

Back on the mainland, driving north from Everett through the prosperous Skagit valley you could be forgiven for thinking you're in Holland. Tulip, daffodil, and iris blooms announce the presence of one of the largest commercial bulb regions in the states. And if you want to combine a little cheese-tasting with your wine-touring in the vicinity, the Washington Cheese Company in Mount Vernon has both an observation and a tasting room.

Bellingham, the major northermost city of Washington, commands an excellent position at the head of Bellingham Bay. A bustling mill community at the turn of the century, the city's older section, known as Old Fairhaven, has been restored to its former glory. Victorian homes and civil buildings contribute to the gracious outlook of this city. The Mount Baker recreation area and the newly created North Cascades National Park are just east of Bellingham.

Blaine, at the U.S.–Canadian border, is a port of entry with its 67-foot-high Peace Arch Monument close by. The Peace Arch, inscribed with the sentiment "Children of a common mother" commemorates the harmonious link between the two countries.

The San Juan Island group in Puget Sound offers a charming respite from big-city life elsewhere. To properly take you back to another time and age, big green-and-white Washington state ferries **left** are the primary means of getting to the island.

171

A bridge rises for a pleasure craft on Lake Washington **above**. One out of six persons in Seattle owns a boat.

The San Juan Islands

Scattered between Puget Sound and Canadian waters are the 172 idyllic getaways of the San Juan Island group. These islands are understandably a mecca for boaters who come to explore the inlets, anchor in the coves, and camp on the beaches. Picture an evening around a blazing driftwood camp fire munching on freshly caught clams, watching the sun set behind the Olympic Mountains; you'll think you've died and gone to heaven. Private boats may land and camp at any of the several marine state parks on islands not reached by ferries. And if desperate seasickness is the bane of your existence there is a regular air service to the San Juans from both Bellingham and Seattle.

Big green and white Washington State Ferries cruise through the islands making several daily round trips from Anacortes to Sidney, Vancouver Island. Apart from the stunning island scenery (including fir and madrona trees that grow right to the water's edge), the water itself holds many surprises. Whales are sometimes sighted in this area, and pods of orcas (killer whales) sometimes escort the ferries past all manner of fishing boats, yachts, motor cruisers, and even occasionally the tenacious little tugs towing long rafts of logs to the mills.

The ferries call at four islands where visitors, with or without cars, have the opportunity to get off, spend a few hours or days exploring, and then catch the next ferry to another island. After leaving Anacortes the first stop is Lopez, a long rather flat island almost entirely given over to poultry and dairy farms. Its quiet country roads, almost devoid of traffic, offer tranquil cycling. Several small resorts scattered along the island's bays and beaches offer cosy accommodation plus all the beachcombing your heart desires.

Smallest of the ferry stops is the heavily wooded Shaw Island. There are no overnight accommodations here other than campsites at Shaw Island Country Park.

Orcas Island is the largest in the tour, dominated by 2,409-foot Mount Constitution. The San Juan archipelago spreads like stepping-stones beneath you. Overnight camping and freshwater fishing are possible at Moran State Park on the east end of the island, and the elegant Rosario Resort, formerly the Moran Mansion, on the west end of the island, caters to the other end of the spectrum.

San Juan, the most populated of the islands, combines rolling terrain and grassy hills on the south with dense forest to the north. Friday Harbor, a small bustling port, is home to a picturesque fishing fleet, a University of Washington Teaching Laboratory specializing in marine biology, and a whale museum. Occu-

pying one of the island's oldest buildings, the whale museum illustrates cetacean behavior and biology and contains some massive whale skeletons. A fascinating exhibit exploring whale song is also featured.

San Juan was British property until 1859, and the National Historical Park commemorates the bloodless and comic Pig War that ended with the island's becoming American. Both English and American camps, each with its blockhouses, barracks, storehouses, blacksmith shop, and cemetery, are preserved—at opposite ends of the island, of course.

Once billed as the tallest building west of the Mississippi, Smith Tower **left** overlooks shops, restaurants and nightlife in historic Pioneer Square, the heart of downtown Seattle.

A Washington state ferry **below** leaves Port Townsend, bound for Keystone, Whidbey Island.

INDEX

PICTURE CREDITS

Rollin R. Geppert: pp.20/21 (top), 25, 26, 27, 38/39 (top right), 42/43 (top), 44/45 (left, bottom), 62, 96/97 (top left, top middle), 98, 99, 100, 113, 116, 117 (bottom right), 120/121 (top), 124/125 (top right), 126/127 137 (middle), 145, 152, 154/155 (left, bottom right), 158 (middle left, top right, bottom right), 159 (middle), 161 (top right, middle), 162, 163, 166 (middle), 167 (top), 169 (top)

Walter Hodges: pp.10/11, 44/45 (top), 108, 136 (bottom), 158 (bottom left), 159 (bottom), 160, 165, 168

T. Olsen: p.172 (top left)

Tom Stilz: p.129 (bottom), 134, 153 (middle), 154/155 (top right), 159 (top left), 170/171 (top right)

Trevor Wood: pp.6, 9, 14, 15, 18, 20/21 (left, right), 29, 30/31 (bottom), 32/33, 34/35, 36, 38/39 (top left, bottom), 46/47, 49, 50/51 (bottom), 56, 57, 58/59 (top left, bottom left), 64/65 (bottom), 86 (bottom), 88, 89, 94/95, 114, 117 (top left), 119, 122/123, 124/125 (left), 128, 129 (top), 130, 132/133, 146/147 (top left, bottom), 149, 150, 153 (top), 156/157

British Columbia Forest Service: pp.22/23 (bottom), 54 (top right, top left), 71 (middle, bottom), 76 (top), 77, 86 (top)

Canadian Government: pp.10/11, 12, 16/17 (right), 22/23 (top), 24, 40/41, 48, 50/51 (top left), 52/53, 54 (bottom left), 58/59 (top right, bottom right), 60, 61, 64/65 (top left, top middle), 66 (bottom), 68, 70 (top, middle), 71 (top), 72/73 (top left), 78, 79, 80/81, 82, 83, 85 (top right, middle), 87, 91, 96/97 (top right), 101, 103, 111, 136 (top), 138, 139, 158 (top left), 161 (top left), 166 (middle), 167 (bottom), 169 (middle), 170/171 (top left, bottom), 172/173 (bottom, right)

City Photo Centre, Victoria B.C.: pp.66 (top), 76 (middle), 140/141

Government of British Colombia: pp.50/51 (top right), 54 (bottom right), 64/65 (top right), 70 (bottom), 72/73 (bottom), 74, 85 (top left), 142, 143

Province of British Colombia Ministry of Health: pp.16/17 (left), 67, 72/73 (top right), 76 (bottom), 84

State of Oregon Travel Information Section: pp.16/17 (top), 30/31 (top), 37, 43/43 (bottom), 92, 102, 104/105, 107, 120/121 (bottom), 124/125 (bottom right), 144, 146/147 (top right), 148

State Tourism: p.137 (top)